MADE FOR GIVING · MADE FOR GIVING · MADE FOR GIVING · MADE FOR GIVING

Gifts from the
KITCHEN

PAMELA WESTLAND

Reader's Digest

THE READER'S DIGEST ASSOCIATION, INC.
Pleasantville, New York • Montreal

A Reader's Digest Book
Conceived, edited, and designed by Marshall Editions

Library of Congress Cataloging in Publication Data

Westland, Pamela
    Gifts from the kitchen / Pamela Westland : [edited and produced by
Marshall Editions Ltd.].
        p. cm. — (Made for giving)
    "A Reader's digest book"—T.p. verso.
    Includes index.
    ISBN 0-89577-955-2
    1. Desserts. 2. Handicraft. 3. Gifts. I. Marshall Editions
Ltd. II. Title. III. Series.
TX773.W475 1997
641.8'6—dc21   96-29921

Printed in Italy

EDITOR LINDSAY MCTEAGUE
ART EDITOR KATHERINE HARKNESS
PHOTOGRAPHER CHRISTINE HANSCOMB
FOOD STYLISTS BRIDGET SARGESON, LINDA MACLEAN
HAND MODEL MICHAELA MOHER
COPY EDITORS JOLIKA FESZT, BEVERLY LEBLANC,
MAGGI MCCORMICK
DTP EDITORS LESLEY GILBERT, KATE WAGHORN
PRODUCTION EDITOR EMMA DIXON
EDITORIAL DIRECTOR SOPHIE COLLINS
ART DIRECTOR SEAN KEOGH
PRODUCTION ROBERT K. CHRISTIE, NIKKI INGRAM

Contents

6 *Introduction*
6 MAKING A SQUARE BOX
8 EQUIPMENT
8 MAKING A ROUND BOX

10 *Small Treats*
12 SCOTTISH SHORTBREAD
16 CINNAMON AND NUT BARS
20 GINGER AND HONEY FAIRINGS
24 LEMON SUGAR-CRYSTAL BUNS
28 CHEESE SHELLS
32 VIENNESE ALPHABET COOKIES
36 COCONUT WREATH COOKIES
40 SPICED GINGERBREAD PEOPLE
44 VANILLA AND PEPPERMINT
   COOKIES

48 *Sweets & Candies*
50 CRANBERRY FUDGE
54 CHOCOLATE COCONUT CANDY
58 A HARVEST OF MARZIPAN
   FRUITS

62 CHOCOLATE RUM TRUFFLES
66 ROSE-PETAL AND ORANGE
   TURKISH DELIGHT
70 FRENCH PISTACHIO NOUGAT
74 SUGAR 'N' SPICE PECANS
78 SUGAR-PASTE LEAVES
82 SUGAR-FROSTED FRUITS

86 *Cakes & Desserts*
88 ROSE-PETAL CAKE
92 CHOCOLATE-PECAN GATEAU
96 OLD-FASHIONED GINGERBREAD
100 BUTTERSCOTCH-TOPPED
   CHEESECAKE
104 ITALIAN CHOCOLATE FRUITCAKE
108 FOUR-LAYER SPICE CAKE
112 THANKSGIVING PUMPKIN PIE
116 LIGHT-AS-AIR CAKE
120 RICH CHRISTMAS FRUITCAKE

124 TEMPLATES
128 INDEX

INTRODUCTION

THERE IS SOMETHING IMMENSELY SATISFYING in handing over an elegant package or box to your host at a party and hearing the thrilled exclamation, "You made this all yourself!"

Creating a lively, innovative wrapping for a gift is as important for the end impression as what's inside the package: your present should look good and taste marvelous. With a little know-how, it is not hard to do.

This book gives comprehensive instructions on both making and packaging, so that your gift has the right blend of the personal touch and the professional finish. All the projects are attainable; even a novice will be rewarded with excellent results. And as your confidence grows, you will find it easy to mix and match the recipes and packaging ideas to create any number of variations. If you're timid about your crafting skills, try the simple fabric wrapping for a Christmas cake on pages 122–23; it couldn't be easier to achieve. And if it's cooking that makes you nervous, start with the Chocolate Rum Truffles on pages 62–63; the delicious end results belie the easy-to-follow recipe.

You can make your own containers – boxes, bags, or paper cones – or buy simple ones to decorate yourself, such as wooden or woven baskets, flowerpots, or pencil holders. The finish on the gifts here is accomplished without having to resort to expensive or elaborate fixings – silver candy wrappers, a few pressed leaves, or a handful of shells gathered on the beach can be made into decorative trimming for any number of simple and delicious things to eat. Above all, enjoy being creative as you perfect the art of giving.

Always follow one set of measurements – either imperial or metric – all the way through a recipe or project.
Many of the recipes make more than you will need to fill the package – this is so you can choose the best ones to give as gifts. ✿

MAKING A SQUARE BOX

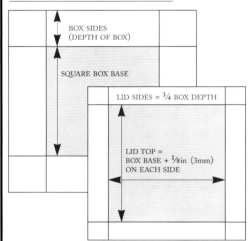

Once you have learned how to make a simple square box, you can adjust the measurements and vary the materials you use to create a satisfying variety of packages.

YOU WILL NEED
Cutting mat, craft knife, ruler, pencil, scissors
Piece of medium-weight cardboard twice as long as it is wide (see sizing guide below)
Double-sided tape, 2 inches (5cm) wide

SIZING BOX BASE & LID

BOX SIDES (DEPTH OF BOX)

SQUARE BOX BASE

LID SIDES = ¾ BOX DEPTH

LID TOP = BOX BASE + ⅛in (3mm) ON EACH SIDE

Note

For a rectangular box use the basic principles outlined above but make the base a rectangle. You can make your box of colored card or cover it in patterned paper (for instructions see pages 114–15, steps 2–7).

TO MAKE A SQUARE BOX 6" x 6" x 1¾" (15 x 15 x 4.5cm)

1 Place a piece of card 10 by 20 inches (25 by 50cm) on the cutting mat. Measure, draw, and cut a square 9½ by 9½ inches (24 by 24cm) to form the base and sides of the box. Measure and draw a line 1¾ inches (4.5cm) in from and parallel to each side. This measurement is the depth of the box. The square in the center, between the four lines, is the base.

2 With a craft knife, score along all the pencil lines, but do not cut through the cardboard at this stage. To make the flaps that will form square corners, cut through one of the two pencil lines at each corner.

3 Measure and cut strips of double-sided tape to cover each of the squares at the corners. With the scored side of the cardboard still uppermost, stick the tape onto each corner.

4 Turn the cardboard over so the scored side is on the mat. Crease along all the scored lines and bring up the sides to form the depth of the box.

5 Peel off the backing from the tape at each corner in turn. With the sticky side inside, overlap the cut section and the side of the box and press the two thicknesses of cardboard together to give neat, square corners.

6 To make the box lid, measure, draw, and cut a square 8¾ by 8¾ inches (22 by 22cm) from the remaining cardboard. Measure and draw a line 1¼ inches (2.75cm) in from and parallel to each of the four sides. This represents the side of the lid. Repeat steps 2 to 7 to finish the lid. ❈

EQUIPMENT

PENCIL, RULER, SCISSORS, CUTTING MAT, craft knife, and double-sided tape are all you need to make most of the packages here. And some of them don't even require this much equipment.

You may already have many of these items at home, but if not, a visit to a craft shop will ensure that you return home with all the tools of the trade. Cardboard in different colors, prettily or strikingly patterned wrapping paper, paints, stencils, ribbons, and bows – all will transform a plain package into a masterpiece.

Add a finishing touch of a tassel handle, a bunch of crystalized roses, or a personalized embossed gift tag. And with the projects here to inspire you, you can let loose your imagination and make gifts to suit any number of your friends.

MAKING A ROUND BOX

A round box and lid is made of four pieces of cardboard – two circles and two thinner strips.

YOU WILL NEED

Cutting mat, craft knife, ruler, pencil, scissors

Piece of medium-weight cardboard for box base and top of lid (see Note below)

Piece of thinner cardboard for sides, as it bends into a neat circle (see Note below)

Drawing compass (or you can use a plate or other round item as a guide)

Packing tape, 2 inches (5cm) wide

Sheet of wrapping paper (see Note below)

Double-sided tape, 2 inches (5cm) wide

SIZING BOX BASE & LID   SIDES

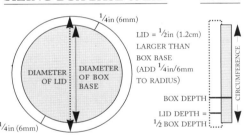

¼in (6mm)

LID = ½in (1.2cm) LARGER THAN BOX BASE (ADD ¼in/6mm TO RADIUS)

DIAMETER OF LID   DIAMETER OF BOX BASE

CIRCUMFERENCE

BOX DEPTH

LID DEPTH = ½ BOX DEPTH

¼in (6mm)

Note

Calculate how much you will need: Medium-weight cardboard width is equal to one diameter plus 1 inch (2.5cm); its length is twice the width. Thinner cardboard length is equal to the circumference of the lid; its width is the sum of the box and lid sides. Wrapping paper length is same as thinner cardboard; width is width of both cardboards plus 2 inches (5cm) for overlap.

TO MAKE A ROUND BOX *7 inches (18cm) in diameter and 2 inches (5cm) deep*

1 Place a piece of medium-weight cardboard 8 by 16 inches (20 by 40cm) on the cutting mat. For the box base, draw a 7-inch (18-cm) circle, using a compass or a round item as a guide. With the craft knife, cut out the circle. For the lid, draw and cut out a circle with a 7½-inch (19-cm) diameter.

2 From a piece of thinner cardboard 3 by 24 inches (8 by 60cm), draw and cut a strip to make the side of the box. It should be 2 by 23 inches (5 by 58cm). This is the depth of the box by the circumference plus 1 inch (2.5cm) for overlap. For the side of the lid cut a strip 1 by 23 inches (2 by 58cm).

3 To make the box base, cut about 36 strips of packing tape ½ inch (1.5cm) long and stick the ends around the rim of a bowl so they are at hand. With the cardboard circle in your hand, stick the strips of tape close together around the circumference, so half of each strip overlaps the edge of the circle.

4 Place the cardboard circle on the work surface so the sticky side of the tape is uppermost. Place the strip for the side of the box upright against the edge of the circle and, starting at one end of the strip, bend over and stick the strips of packing tape to join the two bits.

5 When you reach the other end of the cardboard strip, cut it so that the two ends butt up evenly, then cover the join with a strip of packing tape. Make the lid in the same way as the box, following steps 3 and 4.

6 To cover the box with wrapping paper, follow the instructions on pages 118–19, steps 1–7. You will need a piece of paper about 12 by 24 inches (30 by 60cm). ✿

Small Treats

❉ THE WARM, HOMEY SMELL OF baking is a given with our selection of cookies, and there is an irresistible diversity of recipes, ranging from traditional Scottish shortbread to checkerboard vanilla and peppermint cookies. Add a touch of spice with cinnamon and nut bars, gingerbread people, or ginger and honey fairings sparkling with edible gold leaf, or for a tropical taste try coconut wreath cookies or lemon sugar-crystal buns. Spell out the recipient's name with alphabet cookies for a more personal gift, and try cheese shells packed with sun-dried tomatoes for a savory snack.

There is just as much variety in the packaging ideas too. You can learn how to make cut and folded cardboard boxes, a ribbon-weave panel for a box, a gingham pouch, and a mini carrier bag. You can try your hand at painting and stenciling or stamping ready-made boxes and baskets, or turning some wire and a few trimmings into a glitzy package.

SCOTTISH SHORTBREAD

As traditionally Scottish as its tartan wrappings, this shortbread can be served with morning coffee, a cup of tea, or to accompany a rich and creamy dessert.

RECIPE: Scottish shortbread

Preheat the oven to 350°F (180°C). Lightly grease an 8- by 12-inch (20- by 30-cm) pan with oil and lightly dust it with flour.

RECIPE INGREDIENTS

1 cup (250g) cold unsalted butter, cut into small pieces

2⅔ cups (325g) unsifted all-purpose flour

⅔ cup (140g) superfine sugar

⅓ cup (45g) yellow cornmeal

2 teaspoons (10ml) vanilla extract

Makes 18 biscuits, enough to fill 3 boxes

PACKAGING NEEDS

Ruler, pencil, craft knife, cutting mat, all-purpose glue, cellophane or plastic food wrap, scissors

Piece of medium-weight cardboard 10 by 17 inches (25.5 by 43.5cm)

Plaid wrapping paper

1⅓ yards (1.2m) tartan ribbon, 2½ inches (6.5cm) wide

1 In a mixing bowl, rub the **butter** into the **flour** with your fingertips until it is well blended and the mixture resembles fine bread crumbs.

2 Stir in the **sugar** and **cornmeal,** then add the **vanilla extract.** Turn the mixture onto the countertop and knead for 3 minutes, or until the dough comes together and the cracks disappear.

3 Using the back of a large spoon, press the dough into the prepared pan and flatten the top. Prick the dough all over with a fork.

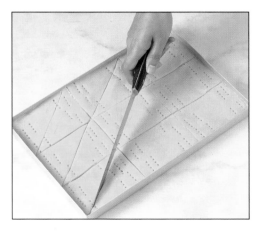

4 Using the back of a knife blade, mark the dough into nine rectangles. Draw a diagonal line across each one to make triangles. ▶

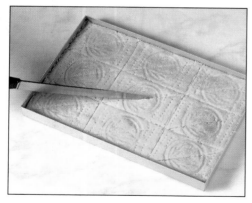

5 If you wish, press a wooden shortbread stamp onto the dough to imprint it with a thistle or other appropriate motif. It may help to put the stamp in the freezer for 30 minutes before you begin; this prevents the dough from sticking to the stamp.

6 Bake the dough in the preheated oven for 30 minutes or until it is golden in color. Leave the shortbread to cool in the pan for about 15 minutes before cutting through the marked lines. Store the shortbread in an airtight container until you giftwrap it. ▪▪

GIFTWRAP: Tartan trimmings

Individually wrapped in cellophane or plaid paper, pieces of shortbread are packed in a recessed box tied with a colorful checked-ribbon bow.

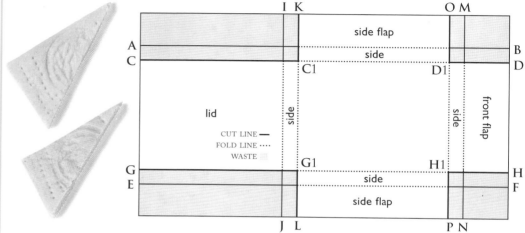

1 Using the template above as a guide, measure and draw two parallel lines 1¼ inches (3.25cm) and 2 inches (5cm), respectively, in from each of the long sides. These are marked A-B and C-D, and E-F and G-H on the template.

2 Measure and draw two parallel lines (I-J) 6¼ inches (16cm) and (K-L) 7 inches (18cm), respectively, in from one of the short sides. Measure and draw the last two parallel lines, (M-N) 2 inches (5cm) and (O-P) 2¾ inches (7cm) in from the opposite side.

3 With the cardboard placed flat on the cutting mat, score along all the marked lines, using the craft knife. These are where the cardboard is to be folded, but take care not to cut through the lines at this stage.

4 Now cut along the inside lines at each corner. In this way you will remove two rectangles 2 by 2¾ inches (5 by 7cm), O-D1-D and P-H1-H, and two rectangles 2 by 7 inches (5 by 18cm), K-C1-C and L-G1-G.

5 Begin folding the box by bending up the outside lines to form the front and side flaps and the lid. Then fold along the inside lines to make the sides and base of the box.

6 To create a recessed box, apply glue to the sides of the front flap and stick it to the side flaps.

7 Wrap each piece of shortbread in cellophane or plastic food wrap. (You do not need to do this if the plaid wrapping paper has a waxed finish.) Then wrap some of the shortbread in the plaid paper.

8 Arrange the shortbread in the box and close the lid. (You will have some pieces left over.) Tie the ribbon around the box, make a bow, and trim the ends.

CINNAMON AND NUT BARS

WITH A MOIST, NUTTY TEXTURE AND CRUNCHY STREUSEL TOPPING, these bars
are packed with cinnamon bundles and a slice of dried orange.

RECIPE INGREDIENTS

¼ cup (60g) lightly salted butter

¾ cup (175g) firmly packed light brown sugar

1 large egg, lightly beaten

1 teaspoon grated orange rind

1¼ cups (150g) unsifted all-purpose flour

1 teaspoon baking powder

1 teaspoon ground cinnamon

½ teaspoon salt

1¾ cups (175g) pecan halves

TOPPING

¼ cup (60g) lightly salted butter

½ cup (60g) unsifted all-purpose flour

¼ cup (60g) firmly packed light brown sugar

½ teaspoon ground cinnamon

1 teaspoon grated orange rind

Makes about 24 bars

PACKAGING NEEDS

Ruler, pencil, craft knife, cutting mat, scissors, tracing paper, masking tape, scrap of cardboard, pin, all-purpose glue, stapler

Piece of medium-weight cardboard 13 by 15 inches (33 by 37.5cm)

Double-sided tape, 2 inches (5cm) wide

Stencil of leaves and fruit (page 18)

Orange and green oil-based stencil sticks or stencil paints

Stencil brush

15 inches (38cm) stiff grosgrain ribbon, 1 inch (2.5cm) wide

6–8 small cinnamon sticks tied into two bundles with raffia

1 dried orange slice (page 26, step 6)

RECIPE: Cinnamon and nut bars

Preheat the oven to 375°F (190°C). Lightly grease an 8-inch (20-cm) square baking pan with vegetable oil, such as sunflower oil.

1 In a medium-sized saucepan, melt the **butter**. Remove it from the heat and set it aside to cool slightly. Stir in the **sugar, egg,** and **orange rind.**

2 Sift the **flour, baking powder, cinnamon,** and **salt** into a mixing bowl, then pour in the sugar mixture.

3 On a chopping board, chop the **pecans** using a sharp knife. Add the nuts to the mixture in the bowl and stir to blend.

4 Turn the mixture into the prepared pan and level the top with a spatula. ▶

5 To make the topping, in a bowl, rub the **butter** into the **flour** with your fingertips and stir in the **sugar, cinnamon,** and **orange rind.** Sprinkle the topping over the mixture in the pan.

6 Bake in the preheated oven for 30 minutes, until the topping is set and browned. Using a sharp knife, cut into 24 bars while still warm. Leave to cool in the pan on a wire rack. ▪▪

GIFTWRAP: Orange ribbons

Two stenciled ribbons of orange fruits and leaves decorate the box, which is made in one piece, then packed with spicy nut bars and cinnamon sticks.

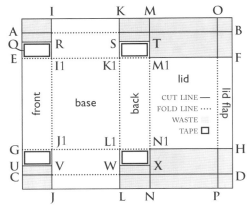

1 Using the template above as a guide, measure and draw with a pencil lines A-B and C-D, 1 inch (2.5cm) in from each of the long sides of the cardboard, and two more, parallel lines, E-F and G-H, 2 inches (5cm) in from each of these. (This is the right side of the box, so make the lines faint.) Measure and draw a line I-J 2 inches (5cm) in from one of the short sides. Then draw a parallel line, K-L, 5 inches (12.5cm) in from that, M-N a further 2 inches (5cm) in, and O-P 5 inches (12.5cm) in. This last line will be 1 inch (2.5cm) from the edge of the cardboard.

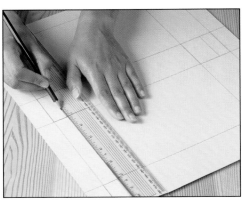

2 There will be four 2-inch (5-cm) squares on the cardboard. Draw a line ³⁄₄ inch (2cm) in from the outer line in each case, Q-R, S-T, U-V, and W-X.

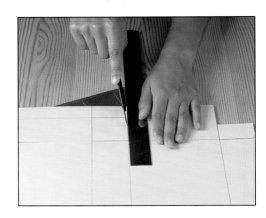

3 Use a craft knife to cut away the corner sections I-R-Q and J-V-U. Cut away the portions marked by points F-M1-T-S-K and H-N1-X-W-L, respectively. Cut through the following: R-I1, V-J1, S-K1, and W-L1.

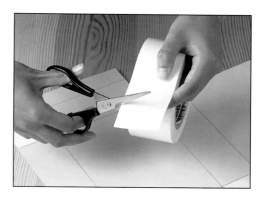

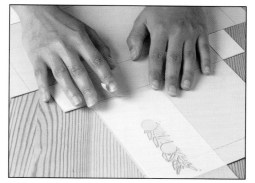

4 Cut four 1¼-inch (3-cm) pieces of double-sided tape, peel off the backing, and stick them on the areas Q-R-I1-E; S-T-M1-K1; U-V-J1-G; and W-X-N1-L1. Cut a liner out of tracing paper for the box. Follow lines E-G-J1-V-W-L1-N1-M1-K1-S-R-I1-E.

5 Trace the stencil at left on tracing paper and cut out the outline, using a craft knife. The stencils form a ribbon pattern from the edge of the lid flap, across the top, back, base, and front of the box. Position the stencil 1¼ inch (3cm) in from one outer edge, F-M1, and parallel to it. Secure it with masking tape.

6 Follow the instructions for the type of stencil color you use. For oil-based sticks rub a little color onto a scrap of cardboard, then rub the brush onto the color. Stencil the leaf and fruit pattern, then mark through the stencil repeat holes with a pin. Reposition the stencil and complete the pattern.

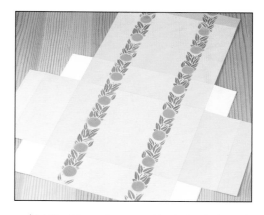

7 Position the stencil 1¼ inch (3cm) in from the opposite edge and color the pattern in the same way. Set aside until the paint has dried. Using a craft knife score along the pencil lines.

8 Fold the box along the scored lines. Starting with the inner sections, peel off the paper on the double-sided tape; press overlapping sections in place. Cut the sides of the front flap diagonally so the box closes easily (see page 16).

9 With the ribbon, make three loops, each smaller than the last; then staple the center. Glue the bow to the top of the box. Place the liner in the box, and stack the bars inside, along with the cinnamon bundles and dried orange slice. 🎁

GINGER AND HONEY FAIRINGS

GOLDEN BROWN AND GLISTENING WITH SPECKS OF EDIBLE GOLD LEAF, these
cookies were traditionally sold at country fairs in Victorian England – hence their name.

RECIPE INGREDIENTS

1 cup (125g) unsifted all-purpose flour

1 teaspoon baking powder

1 teaspoon baking soda

2 teaspoons ground ginger

³/₄ teaspoon cinnamon

¹/₄ teaspoon nutmeg

Dash allspice

¹/₄ cup (60g) cold lightly salted butter, diced

5 tablespoons (60g) superfine sugar

2 tablespoons (30ml) honey, plus extra for brushing

Edible gold leaf, to decorate

Makes about 15 cookies

PACKAGING NEEDS

Wire cutters or pliers, scissors, all-purpose glue, pencil, craft knife, cutting mat, rubber band

10 inches (25cm) medium-gauge florist's wire

2 wire rings, 5 inches (12.5cm) in diameter

4¹/₄ yards (4m) gold metallic ribbon, ¹/₈ inch (3mm) wide

Drawing compass (optional)

Piece of gold-colored cardboard, about 6 by 6 inches (15 by 15cm)

¹/₂ yard (45cm) gold sequin trim, 3¹/₄ inches (8.25cm) wide

Piece of cellophane 12 by 12 inches (30 by 30cm)

Gold-colored gauze or net 20 by 20 inches (50 by 50cm)

RECIPE: Ginger and honey fairings

Preheat the oven to 400°F (200°C). Lightly grease baking sheets with butter.

1 Sift the **flour, baking powder, soda,** and **spices** into a mixing bowl. Add the **butter** and rub it in until the mixture resembles fine crumbs.

2 Stir in the **sugar** and **honey.** Then form the dough into a ball and knead it lightly, in the bowl, until it is smooth and free of cracks.

3 Pull off pieces of the dough and roll them on the countertop with your hand, shaping them into balls the size of a walnut.

4 Place the dough balls 3 inches (7.5cm) apart on the baking sheets – they will spread while baking. Flatten the balls slightly with a fork. ▶

5 Bake in the preheated oven for 6 to 7 minutes, until the cookies are golden brown. Leave the cookies to cool for 2 to 3 minutes, then transfer them to a wire rack using a spatula. While they are still warm, brush the tops of the cookies with melted honey.

6 Tear small pieces of **gold leaf** and, using a small craft brush, press them on top of each cookie. ▪

GIFTWRAP: All that glitters

A package worthy of the most glittering occasion is unwrapped to reveal a wire-frame container covered with sequin trim and full of sparkling cookies.

1 Using wire cutters, cut the florist's wire into three pieces. To make the frame, twist one end of the pieces of wire around one wire ring. Twist the other ends around the other ring so that the rings are 3¼ inches (8.25cm) apart.

2 Cut 1 yard (1m) off the metallic ribbon for the bow. Fix one end of the remaining ribbon onto one of the wire rings with a dab of glue. Bind the ribbon around to cover the ring; repeat for the other ring and the uprights, so the frame is totally covered.

3 With a drawing compass, or using the wire frame as a guide, draw a circle on the back of the cardboard. Using a craft knife, cut it out to fit the base of the frame exactly.

4 Apply some glue to the edge of the cardboard, gold side up, and glue the base of the frame to the board.

5 Working on a small section of the frame at a time, squeeze a little glue onto the outside of the top and bottom rings. Press the sequin trim onto the glued sections and, keeping the trim taut, stick it all around to cover the frame. Allowing for a slight overlap, trim the end of the strip and glue it in place.

6 Press the square of cellophane into the wire-frame container, arrange the cookies inside, and draw the corners of the paper over the top.

7 To wrap the container, place it in the center of the gold net and bring the four corners over the top. Gather the net at the top of the frame and secure with a rubber band.

Note

For a ready-made frame, you can use a drum-shaped wire lampshade frame about 5 inches (12.5cm) in diameter. All you have to do is use wire cutters to cut the bulb holder from the frame and discard the pieces. Then cover the frame with gold metallic ribbon as described.

8 Cut the remaining metallic ribbon in half and place the two pieces together. Tie a bow around the rubber band. ✻

LEMON SUGAR-CRYSTAL BUNS

WITH THEIR SHARP CITRUS TANG and glistening sugar-crystal topping, these buns are light and refreshing. The dried lemon slices packed with them in a wooden basket hint at their flavor.

RECIPE INGREDIENTS

6 tablespoons (90g) lightly salted butter,
at room temperature

½ cup plus 2 tablespoons (125g)
superfine sugar

Grated rind of 1 lemon

1 cup (125g) unsifted all-purpose flour

1 cup (125g) cornstarch

1 teaspoon baking powder

2 large eggs, lightly beaten

1 teaspoon (5ml) lemon juice

About 1 tablespoon (15ml) milk (optional)

About 2 tablespoons large
coffee-sugar crystals

DECORATION

2 lemons, thinly sliced

Makes 12 buns

PACKAGING NEEDS

Rubber gloves, polishing cloth, clear
furniture polish, scissors

Wooden basket with a handle; the one used
here is 6 by 8 inches (15 by 20cm)

Bright yellow and white latex or acrylic
water-based paints

2 small containers, such as foil muffin cups,
for the paint

Medium-grade steel wool

Small piece of sponge

Thin wire

Fresh or dried bay leaves

Piece of green and white checked cotton,
12 by 16 inches (30 by 40cm)

RECIPE: Lemon sugar-crystal buns

Preheat the oven to 425°F (220°C). Lightly grease 12 small muffin tins.

1 In a mixing bowl, beat the **butter** with a wooden spoon until it is light and creamy. Then beat in the **sugar** and **lemon rind** until blended.

2 In another bowl, sift together the **flour, cornstarch,** and **baking powder**. Add the dry ingredients and beaten **eggs** alternately to the butter and sugar, stirring well between additions.

3 Stir in the **lemon juice** and a little **milk,** if needed, so the batter drops easily from the spoon when the spoon is lifted from the bowl.

4 Spoon the batter into the prepared tins and sprinkle the **sugar crystals** on top of each one. ▶

GIFTWRAP: Springtime colors

Painted bright daffodil yellow and decorated with dried lemon slices and scented leaves, this wooden basket will be a practical addition to the kitchen or sunroom.

5 Bake in the preheated oven for about 10 minutes, until the buns are firm and springy to the touch. Leave to cool slightly in the tins, then transfer them to a wire rack to cool completely. Store the buns in an airtight container until you are ready to pack them.

1 Pour a little of the yellow paint into one of the containers. Put on the rubber gloves, break off a piece of steel wool about 2 inches (5cm) square and crumple it into a pad.

2 Dab the steel wool into the paint and, following the grain of the wood, rub in the paint with a few firm strokes. This will both smooth and color the wood in one process.

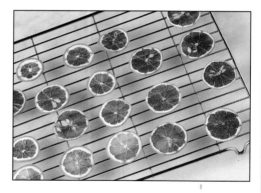

6 To dry the **lemon slices** for the decoration, spread them in a single layer on a wire rack. Place the rack in the oven at 250°F (130°C) for 2 to 3 hours, until the slices are dry. Leave the slices on the rack in a warm dry place overnight. ▪

3 Continue in this way until the basket and handle are painted inside and out. If you would like to leave more of the natural wood showing through, apply the paint thinly and use a clean pad of steel wool to remove some of it. Let the basket dry.

4 Pour a little of the white paint into the other container. Dampen the sponge with water, squeeze out any excess, and dip it into the paint. Dab the sponge all over the basket, leaving some of the yellow color showing through to give a mottled effect.

5 Leave the basket to dry thoroughly. Then, using the polishing cloth, apply the furniture polish and rub it all over the basket. If you would like a glossier finish, apply a second coat of polish.

6 To make the decoration, cut a piece of wire about 6 inches (15cm) long. Thread two or three dried lemon slices and bay leaves alternately on the wire and arrange them into an attractive cluster.

7 Tie the lemon and bay leaf decoration to one side of the basket handle and twist the free ends of the wire together neatly at the back.

8 To finish the edges of the piece of cotton, fold the raw edges over to one side. Then line the basket with the cotton, with the folded sides facing downward.

9 Arrange the buns in the finished painted basket, together with the remaining lemon slices and a few bay leaves. ✽

Note

As an alternative to the wooden basket, you could use a woven basket. Once the lemon sugar-crystal buns have been eaten, the basket, with its liner, can be used for serving bread or rolls.

CHEESE SHELLS

MEDITERRANEAN-STYLE SAVORY SNACKS are perfect to serve with drinks. The scallop shells they are baked in and the shell-topped box continue the seaside theme.

RECIPE INGREDIENTS

1¼ cups (150g) unsifted all-purpose flour

Pinch salt

¾ cup (75g) yellow cornmeal

½ cup (125g) cold unsalted butter

1 cup (125g) freshly and finely grated
Parmesan cheese

2 ounces (60g) sun-dried tomatoes in oil

1 tablespoon chopped fresh basil

2–4 tablespoons (30–60ml) cold water

8 scallop shells, or shell-shaped baking dishes,
or mini tart pans

Makes 8 shell-shaped cheese snacks

PACKAGING NEEDS

Saucer, cotton swab, pencil, tracing paper,
masking tape, piece of cardboard, clear
furniture polish, polishing cloth,
all-purpose glue, waxed paper

Round wooden box with swing handle and
lid; the one used here is 7 inches (18cm) in
diameter and 5½ inches (14cm) deep

Lilac-blue latex paint or acrylic
water-based paint

Pink dry-brush paint or water-based paint

2 small pieces of sponge

Stencils of shell designs (page 31)

Stencil brush

6 or 7 decorative shells

Tissue paper, to line box

RECIPE: Cheese shells

Preheat the oven to 350°F (180°C). Lightly brush eight scrubbed and dried scallop shells with oil and dust them with flour, shaking off the excess.

1 Mix together the **flour, salt,** and **cornmeal** in a mixing bowl and rub in the **butter** with your fingertips until the mixture is like fine crumbs. Stir in the **cheese** with a knife.

2 Pat the **tomatoes** dry with a paper towel and chop them finely. Add them to the butter mixture.

3 Stir in the **basil** and enough **water** to make a dough. Knead the dough in the bowl until it is smooth, then divide it into eight equal portions.

4 Roll out each portion of dough on a floured surface to about the size of a shell. Lightly press the dough into each of the prepared shells and trim the edges with a sharp knife. ►

5 Stand the shells on baking sheets and bake them in the preheated oven for 20 minutes, or until they are golden brown.

6 Leave the pastry in the shells to cool for about 15 minutes. Loosen around the edges with a knife and carefully turn them out onto a wire rack until completely cool. Store them between layers of waxed paper in an airtight tin. ▪▪

GIFTWRAP: A shell collection

The cheese shells are packed in a wooden box with a swing handle, reminiscent of a beach bucket. The stenciled shell decoration hints at what might be inside.

1 Remove the box lid and set it aside. Pour a little of the lilac-blue paint onto a saucer. Squeeze the sponge and lightly dampen it with water, squeezing out any excess. Then dip the sponge into the paint.

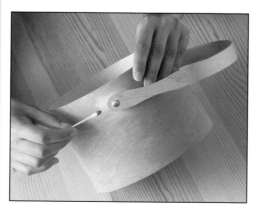

3 Use a cotton swab dipped in paint to reach the difficult areas around the handle. Allow the paint to dry.

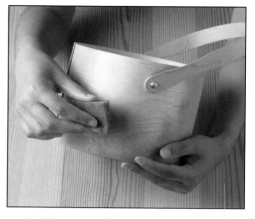

2 Using stroking movements and working in the direction of the grain, apply the paint to the side and base of the box.

4 Turn the box upside-down and mark the center front with a pencil to make it easier to position the stencil.

5 Trace and cut out the shell stencils. Position the scallop shell on the center front of the box and anchor it with masking tape. Use a stencil brush to apply the pink dry-brush paint, following the directions on the product. If you are using water-based paint, apply it with a sponge as before, dabbing off any excess on the cardboard. Allow the paint to dry.

8 Glue a cluster of shells on the center of the lid.

6 Work out where you want to place the other shell stencils around the box. Position the next one with masking tape and apply the paint as before. Allow the paint to dry before moving the stencil and painting the rest.

9 Line the box with crumpled tissue paper and carefully place the shells inside. If it is likely to be a while before the box is opened, put waxed paper between each one. ✤

7 Polish the lid and handle of the box, and when all the shell patterns are dry, polish the box, using two applications of polish if you prefer a glossier finish.

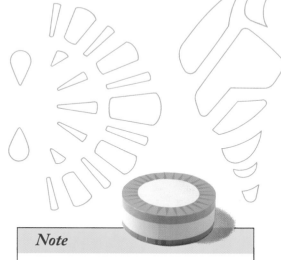

Note

If you cannot find a box with a handle, you could make a round box following the general instructions on pages 8–9, or use a ready-made papier-mâché one.

VIENNESE ALPHABET COOKIES

MAKE THESE SHAPED COOKIES TO SPELL OUT A NAME OR A SEASONAL GREETING,
or make them all in the more traditional letter "S" shape.

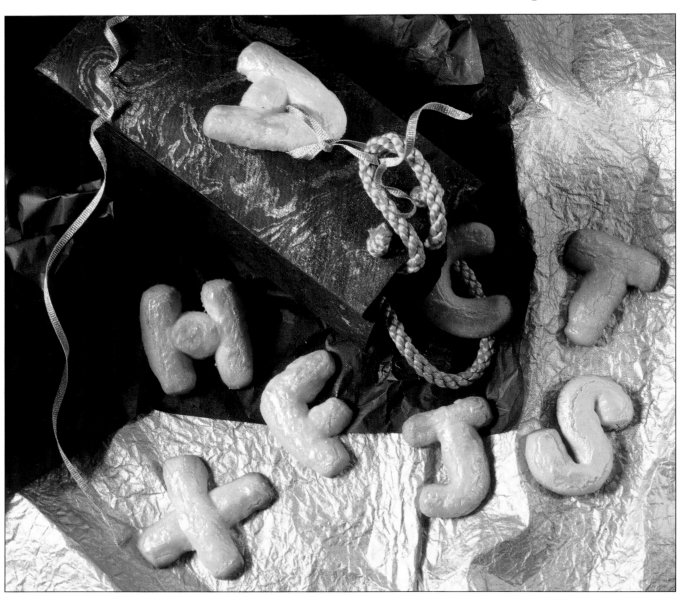

RECIPE INGREDIENTS

10 tablespoons (150g) lightly salted butter, softened

¾ cup (75g) confectioners sugar, plus extra for dusting

Pinch salt

Grated rind of ½ orange

2 large egg yolks, lightly beaten, plus one, lightly beaten, for glazing

1¾ cups (215g) unsifted all-purpose flour

Makes about 26 cookies

PACKAGING NEEDS

Ruler, paper glue, hole punch, scissors, tape

Piece of medium-weight wrapping paper; for the dimensions used here 9¾ by 13¾ inches (25 by 35cm)

Rectangular box to use as a model; the one used here measures 6" x 4" x 1⅞" (15 x 10 x 4.75cm)

20 inches (50cm) thick shiny cord, for handles

Edible gold powder (optional)

Small craft brush (optional)

Cellophane or a plastic bag, for packing cookies

One cookie, the initial of the recipient

½ yard (45cm) gold metallic ribbon, ⅛ inch (3mm) wide

RECIPE: Viennese alphabet cookies
Oven temperature 375°F (190°C). Line baking sheets with waxed paper.

1 Put the **butter** into a mixing bowl. Sift in the **confectioners sugar** and **salt**, add the **orange rind** and two **egg yolks**, and beat, using an electric beater or wooden spoon, until smooth.

2 Sift in the **flour** and mix to form a firm dough. Knead until the dough is smooth and free of cracks. Wrap the dough in aluminum foil and chill in the refrigerator for at least 4 hours, or overnight.

3 Preheat the oven and prepare the baking sheets. Unwrap the dough, sprinkle it and the countertop with sifted confectioners sugar, and roll the dough to a thickness of ⅜ inch (1cm). Cut the dough into strips ⅜ inch (1cm) wide.

4 Gather any trimmings together, roll them out again, and cut more strips. Using your fingers, roll the strips lightly on the countertop to make them round. ▶

5 Draw two lines 2 inches (5cm) apart on baking parchment. Use the lines as a guide to shape the strips into letters; the dough is soft and larger shapes will break. Press the dough gently to smooth over any seams. Using a spatula, place the letter shapes well apart on the baking sheets and brush the tops with the extra egg yolk.

6 Bake in the preheated oven for 10 minutes, or until the cookies are golden brown. Leave them to cool and firm up slightly, then transfer them to a wire rack to cool completely. ▪▪

GIFTWRAP: Bags of gold

A stylish bag made of marbled paper with golden cord handles is personalized with a gold-brushed alphabet cookie for decoration.

1 Fold one long edge of the paper ½ inch (1.5cm) to the wrong side. Glue in place.

3 Fold under the excess paper at the bottom of the box, as you would when wrapping a present, and glue the overlaps in place. Carefully remove the box from the bag.

2 Place the paper right side down on the work surface. Place the box on the paper, with its top edge even with the folded edge of the paper. Wrap the paper around the box and glue the overlap.

4 Using the hole punch, make two holes on each side of the bag, close to the top and about 1½ inches (4cm) apart.

5 Cut the cord in half and bind the four ends with tape to prevent them from fraying. From the inside, thread the two ends of one length of cord through the punched holes on one side of the bag.

6 Knot the ends on the outside of the bag, peel off the tape, and trim the ends. Make the other handle in the same way.

7 If you wish, brush the cookies with the edible gold powder, using a small craft brush.

8 To prevent the cookies from staining the marbled bag, use the cellophane to make a smaller bag to put them in. Reserve one cookie for the decoration. Seal the top of the cellophane bag with tape and place it in the outer bag.

9 Tie the reserved cookie to one of the handles on the outer bag, using the metallic ribbon.

COCONUT WREATH COOKIES

As decorative as they are delicious, these cookies also make attractive Christmas tree ornaments. You can sow the seeds of the idea by tying some with narrow red or green ribbons.

RECIPE INGREDIENTS

1 cup (125g) unsifted all-purpose flour

5 tablespoons (60g) superfine sugar

½ cup packed (60g) shredded coconut

*2 tablespoons (30g) lightly salted butter,
at room temperature*

1 large egg, lightly beaten

About 2 tablespoons (30ml) milk

Red and green candied cherries, to decorate

*2 cookie cutters, 2 inches (5cm) and 1 inch
(2.5cm) in diameter*

Makes about 25 cookies

PACKAGING NEEDS

*Scissors, all-purpose glue, iron, needle and
thread, small plastic bag*

*Wooden box, sold as a desk tidy; the
one used here is 3½" x 3½" x 4¾"
(9 x 9 x 12cm)*

Fine sandpaper

Red matte paint

Small paintbrush

*Piece of thick cardboard 3 by 3½ inches
(7.5 by 9cm)*

*Piece of cotton gingham 21 by 21 inches
(53 by 53cm)*

*Double-sided tape, 2 inches
(5cm) wide*

*½ yard (45cm) thin cord in each of two
coordinated shades*

RECIPE: Coconut wreath cookies

Preheat the oven to 375°F (190°C). Line baking sheets with parchment paper.

1 In a mixing bowl, combine the **flour, sugar, coconut, butter,** and **egg** using a wooden spoon. Stir in just enough **milk** to make a firm dough.

2 On a lightly floured surface, roll out the dough to a thickness of ¼ inch (6mm). Cut out circles with a 2-inch (5-cm) round cookie cutter, pressing the cutter firmly straight down into the dough. Do not twist or turn the cutter, or the shape will be spoiled.

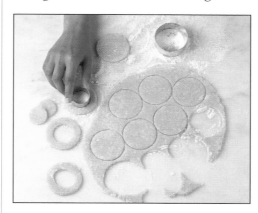

3 Using a 1-inch (2.5-cm) round cookie cutter, cut out the middles of the circles in the same way. Gather up the trimmings, roll them out again, and cut out more rings. You will have about 25 rings.

4 Using a small sharp knife, cut the **cherries** into little crescent-shaped pieces. ▶

5 Place the dough rings on the prepared baking sheets and decorate with the pieces of cherry, alternating the red and green.

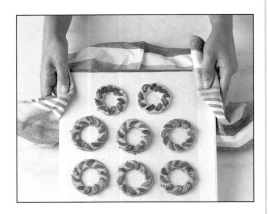

6 Bake the rings in the preheated oven for about 12 minutes, or until they begin to turn light brown at the edges. Let the cookies cool for 5 minutes on the baking sheets, then transfer to a wire rack with a metal spatula. ▪▪

GIFTWRAP: In the bag

The colorful coconut rings are presented together with two lasting gifts, a purchased and painted wooden box and a cotton gingham bag.

1 Lightly sandpaper the surface of the wooden box to provide a base for the paint, then dust it. Paint the outside of the box with the red paint and let it dry. Apply a second coat if necessary, and let it dry.

3 With the fabric right side down, peel off the covering strips and press the cardboard quickly and firmly onto the center of the panel. Fold over the sides of the fabric and stick them down on the back of the cardboard.

2 Cut a piece of gingham 4 by 5 inches (10 by 12.5cm) and cover the wrong side with double-sided tape. Position the cardboard in the center and draw around it. Cut away quarter-circle shapes from the corners of the fabric up to the corners, to reduce bulk when the edges are turned in.

4 Stick the cloth panel onto the center of one side of the box, and glue one of the cookies to it, using the all-purpose glue.

5 To make the bag, cut a piece of fabric 16 inches (40cm) square. Turn ¼ inch (6mm) to the wrong side along each side of the fabric and iron in place. For the top of the bag, take one side of the material and turn over 2¼ inches (6cm) to the wrong side. Sew a hem, either by hand or using a sewing machine.

6 With the right sides together, and the hem at the top, fold the bag in half so the two side edges meet. Leaving a ¼-inch (6-mm) seam, sew the edges together, to make the center back of the bag.

7 To finish the bag, sew a ¼-inch (6-mm) seam along the bottom. Turn the bag right side out.

8 Tie a knot in each end of both lengths of cord. Hold the two pieces of cord together and find the middle point. Sew the cords to the back of the bag, over the center back seam and even with the top hem.

9 Place the plastic bag inside the cotton one and insert it into the box. Fill the bag with cookies and tie the cords around the top. ❄

Note

You could present the cookies in the checked bag alone, or make a cardboard box of dimensions similar to those of the wooden one and either paint it red or cover it with red giftwrap. For a seasonal gift, turn the cookies into Christmas tree decorations by looping red or green ribbon through the central hole of each wreath.

SPICED GINGERBREAD PEOPLE

GINGERBREAD MEN AND WOMEN ARRANGED in a circle in a polka-dot box make a fun gift. Include the cutters, and these figures can become part of the family.

RECIPE INGREDIENTS

*1½ cups (175g) unsifted
all-purpose flour*

Pinch salt

½ teaspoon baking soda

1 teaspoon ground ginger

½ teaspoon ground cinnamon

½ teaspoon ground allspice

6 tablespoons (90g) unsalted butter, softened

2 tablespoons soft dark brown sugar, packed

¼ cup (60ml) molasses

3 tablespoons (45ml) milk

*Two 4-inch (10-cm) gingerbread
cookie cutters*

FROSTING

½ cup (60g) confectioners sugar, sifted

2-3 teaspoons (10-15ml) lemon juice or water

Assorted food colorings

Makes at least 8 cookies

PACKAGING NEEDS

*3 saucers, scissors, all-purpose glue, drawing
compass (optional), craft knife, cutting mat*

*Used wooden cheese box, about 14 inches
(35cm) in diameter, or make a round cardboard
box, following the instructions on pages 8–9*

White latex paint

¾-inch (2-cm) paintbrush

2 small cans of blue and green latex paint

Small piece of sponge

*1 yard (1m) gossamer ribbon,
2½ inches (6.5cm) wide*

*½ yard (45cm) double-faced satin ribbon,
⅜ inch (8mm) wide*

*Piece of heavy cardboard, about 15 by 15
inches (38 by 38cm)*

*30 inches (75cm) paper ribbon,
3½ inches (9cm wide)*

Tissue paper, to line box

RECIPE: Spiced gingerbread people

Oven temperature 375°F (190°C). Lightly brush baking sheets with oil.

1 Sift the **flour, salt, baking soda,** and **spices** into a bowl. In a separate bowl, beat the **butter, sugar,** and **molasses** until well blended. Add the dry ingredients and **milk** alternately to the butter mixture and stir to make a dough.

2 Wrap the dough in waxed paper and chill it in the refrigerator for at least 2 hours. It is slightly sticky, but will become firmer.

3 Preheat the oven. On a lightly floured surface, roll out the dough to a thickness of ¼ inch (6mm).

4 Using the gingerbread cookie cutters, cut out four men and four women shapes for the gift. Reroll the trimmings and cut some more shapes if you wish. ►

5 Arrange the cookies on the prepared baking sheets. Bake them in the oven for 10 to 12 minutes, until they are beginning to darken at the edges. Let them cool slightly on the baking sheet, then transfer them to a wire rack.

6 To decorate the cookies, mix the **confectioners sugar** to a stiff paste with the **lemon juice** or **water**. Color it as you wish and spoon it into a decorating bag fitted with a fine tip. Pipe features or the outlines of clothes or jewelry onto the gingerbread people. ∷

GIFTWRAP: Family circle

Pack the gingerbread family ring in a shallow wooden box painted with polka dots, and tie on one of the cookie cutters as a fun extra.

1 Paint the outside of the box base and lid with white latex paint and set them aside to dry.

3 Using a pair of scissors, cut out a circle about 2 inches (5cm) in diameter from the piece of sponge. This is the stamp for the white polka dots on the lid. Save the rest of the sponge for the next step.

2 Put a little of each of the paints in a small saucer or container. Then paint the base of the box green and the lid blue, and leave them to dry.

4 Dip a small piece of sponge in the blue paint and dab it onto the base to create a slightly marbled effect. Let the paint dry. If you wish, you can marble the lid with green paint if you want to omit the white dots.

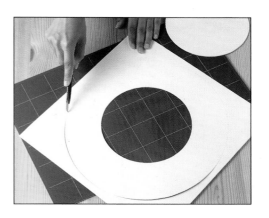

5 Pour a little white latex paint into a saucer. Lightly dip the sponge circle into the paint and stamp circles randomly all over the lid. Set the lid aside to dry.

6 Tie the wide gossamer ribbon in a bow and glue it to the lid. Trim the ends into "V" shapes. Thread the narrow ribbon through one of the gingerbread cutters and tie the cutter to the bow.

7 Using a drawing compass, or two plates as a guide, draw a cardboard circle with an outer diameter of 12 inches (30cm) and an inner diameter of 9 inches (23cm) to fit in the box. Cut around the edges of the circles with a craft knife on a cutting mat.

8 Open the paper ribbon to its full width, then wrap it around the cardboard to cover the circle entirely. Use a piece of tape or glue to secure the ends.

9 In a small dish, mix a teaspoon of confectioners sugar into a paste with a couple of drops of water. Use this to stick the gingerbread men and women alternately around the ring. Line the box with crumpled tissue paper, and place the ring inside. 🎁

Note

For a more "fairytale" presentation for a child, buy a stamp, for example, one of a teddy bear, and use it to decorate the lid in place of the bolder white polka dots.

Vanilla and Peppermint Cookies

The contrasting colors of the green and cream checked cookies are echoed in the woven ribbon pattern that decorates the top of the two-tone cardboard box.

RECIPE INGREDIENTS

3 cups plus 2 tablespoons (400g) unsifted all-purpose flour

1¼ cups (250g) sugar

½ teaspoon salt

½ cup (125g) lightly salted butter, softened

2 large eggs, plus one for binding

2 teaspoons (10ml) vanilla extract

3 drops edible yellow food coloring, or as desired

1 teaspoon (5ml) peppermint extract

8–10 drops edible green food coloring, or as desired

Makes about 24 cookies

PACKAGING NEEDS

Ruler, pencil, craft knife, cutting mat, scissors, staple gun or stapler, tape, all-purpose glue

Piece of cream stiff cardboard 10 by 10 inches (25 by 25cm), for the box

Piece of green stiff cardboard 16 by 16 inches (40 by 40cm), for the lid

Double-sided tape, ⅜ inch (1cm) wide and 2 inches (5cm) wide

1¼ yards (1.25m) each cream and green stiff grosgrain ribbon, ⅞ inch (2.25cm) wide

Tracing paper, for lining

RECIPE: Vanilla and peppermint cookies
Oven temperature 400°F (200°C). Line baking sheets with waxed paper.

1 In a mixing bowl, beat together the **flour, sugar, salt, butter,** and **two eggs** until the mixture comes together. Divide the mixture in half and put one half into another bowl.

2 Add the **vanilla** and **yellow food coloring** to half the dough and knead until the color is well blended. Form into a ball. Repeat with the **peppermint extract** and **green coloring**. Wrap the balls separately in plastic food wrap and chill for at least 1 hour.

3 Roll out each piece of dough between waxed paper until ⅜ inch (1cm) thick. Using a clean ruler as a guide, cut the dough into strips ⅜ inch (1cm) wide. You need 12 strips of one color, 13 of the other.

4 Place five dough strips on the countertop, alternating the colors. Brush the surface with beaten egg. Place another layer of strips on top, with green over yellow and so on. ►

5 Continue alternating layers to build up a five-layer checkerboard. Pat the dough block firmly with your hands, then form any remaining dough into blocks. Place the blocks in the freezer for about 30 minutes. Preheat the oven. Using a sharp knife, cut the blocks into slices ½ inch (1.5cm) thick.

6 Place the dough slices on the baking sheets and bake in the preheated oven for 10 to 12 minutes, until the cookies are light brown at the edges. Leave the cookies to cool slightly, then transfer them to a wire rack. ▪▪

GIFTWRAP: Checked ribbons

The woven ribbon panel gives a plain, uncovered gift box an elegant look. And when the cookies are finished, it will make a pretty container for other things.

1 To make the base of the box, draw a 9½-inch (24-cm) square on the cream cardboard. Measure and draw lines 1¾ inches (4.5cm) in from each of the four sides. Then, using a craft knife on a cutting mat, cut around the outer lines.

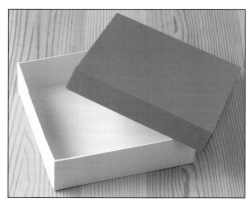

3 Make the box and lid, following the general instructions on pages 6–7.

2 For the box lid, draw an 8⅛-inch (20.5-cm) square on the green board. Measure and draw lines 1 inch (2.5cm) in from each of the four sides. Cut around the outer lines as before.

4 To make the decorative panel, cut a 6⅛-inch (15.5-cm) square of green cardboard. Measure and draw lines 1 inch (2.5cm) in from each side. Cut out the center part, leaving a frame.

5 Cut two strips of the narrow double-sided tape to fit the edge of the frame. Stick the strips onto the back of the frame close to the outer edges on two opposite sides. Mark the center of the frame with a pencil.

6 Cut five 5½-inch (14-cm) strips of the ribbon in one color (cream in the photographs). Peel off the covering from the tape. Starting at the marked center, place the ribbon strips close together and parallel across the back of the frame. Press the ribbon edges onto the tape.

7 Cut five 5½-inch (14-cm) strips of green ribbon and weave each one alternately under and over the cream ones. It may help to secure each ribbon individually with tape on the back of the frame.

8 Stick four strips of wide double-sided tape around the back of the frame to cover the ribbon ends. Peel off the covering, and stick the panel onto the box lid.

9 Place the two remaining strips of ribbon one on top of the other and make a loop about 3 inches (7.5cm) long. Holding it in the center, make two more loops, each one smaller than the last, to form a six-loop bow.

10 Staple through the center of the bow and trim the ribbon ends. Glue the bow at an angle across one corner of the box lid. Line the box with tracing paper, fill it with the cookies, and cover them with a square of tracing paper. 🎁

Sweets & Candies

🎁 ANY OF THESE SWEET TREATS will make a welcome gift, perhaps as a birthday token or a personal thank you. They range from the instant pleasure of melt-in-the-mouth cranberry fudge and chocolate truffles to the longer-lasting chewiness of candied pecans, Turkish delight, and pistachio nougat. Test your artistic skills by making small sugar-paste leaves or modeling miniature marzipan fruits. For no-cook delicacies try sugar-frosted fruits or chocolate coconut candies.

Our gift-packing ideas, which will add immeasurably to the elements of surprise and delight, include the step-by-step transformation of household items such as wire baskets, metal cans, flowerpots, and preserving jars into stylish and decorative containers. In addition, there are instructions for making a large-scale matchbox and a simple colored paper cone and for burnishing a ready-made wooden box to give an antique look.

CRANBERRY FUDGE

A PERFECT WINTER HOLIDAY GIFT, this fudge combines a delightful
sweetness with the sharp taste of the bright seasonal berries.

RECIPE INGREDIENTS

1 cup (90g) cranberries

4¼ cups plus 2 tablespoons (875g) granulated cane sugar

⅔ cup (150ml) milk

¼ cup (60g) lightly salted butter

1 teaspoon (5ml) maple syrup

⅔ cup (160ml) sweetened condensed milk

1 teaspoon (5ml) vanilla extract

Makes about 1¾ pounds (875g)

PACKAGING NEEDS

Tracing paper, tape, pencil, craft knife, cutting mat, masking tape, press cloth, iron, pins, hole punch, pen

Small rectangular wire container; the one used here measures 3½ by 5½ inches (9 by 14cm)

Tulip stencil and heart design (page 52)

White or cream cotton table napkin, about 12 by 12 inches (30 by 30cm)

Red and green fabric paints

Small dish, to use as palette

Stencil brush

Small piece of white cardboard 2½ by 2½ inches (6 by 6cm)

½ yard (45cm) cranberry-colored double-faced satin ribbon, ⅛ inch (3mm) wide

RECIPE: Cranberry fudge

Lightly grease a 7-inch (18-cm) square baking pan with vegetable oil.

1 Steam the **cranberries** over a saucepan of boiling water set over medium heat for 2 to 3 minutes, or until they are bright red. Remove them from the heat and allow to cool.

2 Put the **sugar, milk, butter,** and **syrup** into a large, heavy-bottomed saucepan and stir over low heat until the sugar has dissolved. Increase the heat and bring to a boil, stirring all the time. Add the **condensed milk.**

3 Boil the mixture, still stirring, until it registers 240°F (116°C) on a candy thermometer. Alternatively, drop some of the mixture into a cup of ice-cold water: it should form a soft ball that is easily flattened when pressed.

4 Remove the saucepan from the heat and stir in the cranberries and the **vanilla extract.** Continue stirring with a wooden spoon until the mixture begins to thicken. ▶

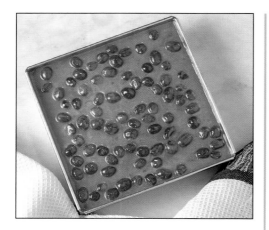

5 Pour the fudge into the prepared pan and let it cool and set for about 15 minutes.

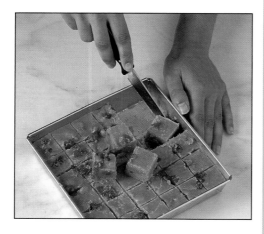

6 Using a small sharp knife, mark cutting lines on the fudge in 1-inch (2.5-cm) squares. Set the fudge aside to cool completely, then cut it and store the pieces in an airtight container until you are ready to giftwrap them. ▪▪

GIFTWRAP: In holiday mood

The simple wire container with its heart-shaped decoration will have a number of practical uses long after the confectionery has been eaten.

1 Place the tracing paper on the work surface and arrange the squares of fudge on it in a double layer to fit into the container (you will have some fudge left over). Wrap the package, securing the edges with tape.

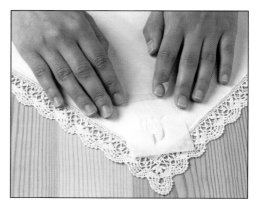

2 On tracing paper, draw around the stencils below and cut them out with a craft knife on a cutting mat. Place the small tulip at one corner of the napkin and secure it with masking tape.

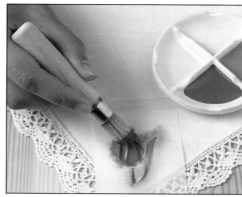

3 Pour a little paint into the dish. Working with a nearly dry brush, stencil the design in each corner. Let each color dry for a few minutes before applying the next.

4 Then, securing the stencil as before, stencil the larger motif close to the center of each edge of the napkin. Protecting the fabric with a press cloth, iron over the design with a cool iron to fix the paint.

5 Place the napkin right side up and fold the two sides to the center. Press along the creases. Place the napkin folded side down and lay the package of fudge on top.

6 Wrap the package so that one edge of the napkin rests on the edge of the fudge package. Fold in the two ends and secure with pins.

7 Place the napkin package in the container and open out the two corners on top to reveal one of the decorations along the napkin edge.

8 Using the stencil you have made, cut out a heart shape from the white cardboard. Punch a hole in the gift tag and thread the ribbon through it. Write a message on one side and stencil a tulip bud and leaf on the other, then tie the card to the container. 🎁

Note

You can also pack the fudge in other kitchen containers such as small baking pans, or you could make a rectangular box following the general instructions for making a square box on pages 6–7.

CHOCOLATE COCONUT CANDY

THESE CHOCOLATY REFRIGERATOR CANDIES look as if they have been lightly dusted with fine snow.
They are simple enough for young children to make with supervision.

RECIPE INGREDIENTS

½ cup (125g) unsalted butter

7 ounces (215g) semisweet chocolate, broken into pieces

⅔ cup (60g) shredded or flaked coconut

1 cup (75g) regular or quick-cooking rolled oats, uncooked

Confectioners sugar, sifted, for dusting

Small confectionery fluted cups

Makes about 24 candies

PACKAGING NEEDS

String, scissors, ruler, pencil, craft knife, cutting mat, all-purpose glue

Used 1-pound (500-g) food canister, washed and thoroughly dried

Piece of corrugated cardboard, to wrap around canister (see step 1)

Double-sided tape, 2 inches (5cm) wide

Piece of medium-weight cardboard, about 12 by 12 inches (30 by 30cm), for base and lid

Ball of coarse string or paper cord

4 seed heads such as poppy, for decoration

Gold craft powder (optional)

Small craft brush (optional)

Tracing paper (optional)

RECIPE: Chocolate coconut candy
Line baking sheets with waxed paper.

1 Melt the **butter** and **chocolate** in a heatproof bowl set over a saucepan of boiling water. (It is not necessary to put the saucepan over direct heat.)

2 As it melts, stir the butter and chocolate mixture with a wooden spoon, beating it until it is well blended and glossy.

3 Remove the bowl from the saucepan and dry the base with a dish towel. Stir in the **coconut** and **oatmeal,** then set aside until the mixture cools.

4 Drop heaped teaspoonfuls of the mixture onto the lined baking sheets. Use another teaspoon to move the mixture off the spoon and to help shape walnut-sized balls. Put the sheets of candies into the refrigerator to set for about 1 hour. ▶

5 Place the candies on the countertop and sift the **confectioners sugar** over them to give a light dusting.

6 Carefully place the candies in individual confectionery cups, taking care not to shake off too much confectioners sugar as you do so. ▪▪

GIFTWRAP: All strung up

A metal food container wrapped in corrugated cardboard and finished with a string-covered lid and base has an informal, modern look that is just right.

1 Using a piece of string, measure the circumference of the container. Then use a ruler to measure the height. Cut a piece of corrugated cardboard to fit the container exactly when it is wrapped. The container here was covered with a piece of cardboard 5¾ by 12 inches (14.5 by 30cm).

2 Cut a piece of double-sided tape exactly the length of the container (in this case 5¾ inches/ 14.5cm) and stick it onto the can.

3 Peel the backing strip off the tape and press one edge of the corrugated cardboard halfway across the strip. Wrap the cardboard tightly around the container and press the second edge onto the tape to meet the first one. Carefully measure the diameter of the container now that it is wrapped in cardboard. The one here measures 4 inches (10cm) wide.

4 To make the base and lid, cut two cardboard circles with the exact diameter of the covered can, using a craft knife on a cutting mat. Then cut two side strips 1 inch (2.5cm) wide and 12 inches (30cm) long. Following the instructions on pages 8–9 for making a round box, make the boxlike base and the lid in the same way.

5 To cover the cardboard base and lid (which are identical) with string or cord, spread the glue over the center. Start in the middle with a tight coil of string and press it on the glue. Applying more glue as you work, coil and press the string until the top and sides are covered. Cut off and glue the string end in place.

6 Spread glue over the bottom and side of the string-covered base and press the container firmly onto it.

7 Glue the seed heads onto the lid, and brush them with gold craft powder if you wish.

8 Fill the canister with the candies, and put on the lid. If you wish, you can cut circles of tracing paper to place between the layers of candies. 🎁

Note

To strike a brighter note, try using corrugated cardboard in primary colors. You could also experiment by making the corrugations run horizontally instead of vertically.

A HARVEST OF MARZIPAN FRUITS

REALISTIC APPLES, PEARS, ORANGES, AND BANANAS painted with food coloring and studded with clove stems are presented in a twig-topped box.

RECIPE INGREDIENTS

2½ cups (500g) sugar

⅔ cup (150ml) water

Pinch cream of tartar

2 cups (375g) blanched almonds, finely ground

2 large egg whites

¾ cup (90g) confectioners sugar, plus extra for attaching fruit (see page 61, step 7)

Red, green, orange, yellow, and brown edible food colorings, paste or powder

Few drops of almond extract

Whole cloves for stems

Makes about 1½ pounds (750g) fruits

PACKAGING NEEDS

Rubber or cotton household gloves, clear furniture polish, polishing cloth, all-purpose glue, ruler, pencil, scissors

Wooden box with a lid; the one used here is 6" x 4½" x 2" (15 x 11.5 x 5cm)

Orange latex or acrylic water-based paint

Gold paint

Medium-brown wood stain

3 small containers, such as foil muffin cups

Medium-grade steel wool

Small, bare forked twig

Waxed paper, to line box

Small confectionery fluted cups

RECIPE: A harvest of marzipan fruits

Lightly brush a baking sheet with a lightly flavored oil, such as sunflower oil.

1 Put the **sugar** and **water** into a large, heavy-based saucepan and stir continuously over low heat until the sugar has dissolved. Bring the syrup to a boil without stirring.

2 Dissolve the **cream of tartar** in a tablespoon of cold water, stir it into the syrup, and continue boiling until the temperature reaches 240°F (116.°C). Remove the pan from the heat and beat the syrup with a wooden spoon until it turns opaque.

3 Stir in the **ground almonds** and **egg whites.** Return the saucepan to low heat and stir for 2 to 3 minutes.

4 Pour the mixture onto the baking sheet, sift over the **confectioners sugar,** and stir it in with a spatula. Allow the paste to cool, then knead it, sifting on a little more confectioners sugar if necessary, until it is pliable. ▶

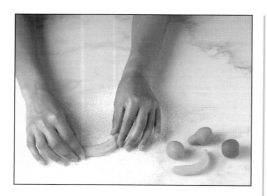

5 Divide the paste into quarters. Add a dab of paste or pinch of powder **food coloring** on each one. Knead until uniformly colored, adding more color as desired. Sift confectioners sugar onto the counter, and mold small pieces of the paste to represent the different fruit.

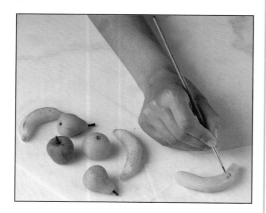

6 Dilute the food coloring in **almond extract** and brush it over the bananas, apples, and pears to add shading. Lightly press the oranges over a fine grater to add texture. Press cloves into the fruit to make stems and bottoms. Leave the fruit to dry, then store them in an airtight container. ▪

GIFTWRAP: Golden glow

A wooden box painted in orange and brown and streaked with gold is decorated with a miniature "tree" of marzipan fruits.

1 Pour a little of the orange and gold paints and the brown wood stain into separate containers.

2 Put on the rubber gloves. Tear off three pieces of steel wool, each about 2 inches (5cm) square, and shape them into pads.

3 Dab one of the steel-wool pads into the orange paint and, going with the grain of the wood, work in the paint with long, firm strokes to cover the sides and base of the box.

4 Without waiting for the paint to dry, rub gold paint over the orange. Then, again without allowing the paint to dry, rub in the wood stain and then another layer of gold paint.

5 Leave this final coat to dry, then rub over the box lightly with a small pad of clean steel wool. Repeat the same paint sequence on the lid and let it dry.

6 Polish the box and the lid with one or two coats of furniture polish, depending on how glossy you want the finish to be.

7 Glue the forked twig to the lid and let dry. Press on some of the marzipan fruits. Make a thick paste with a little confectioners sugar and water and use this to "glue" the fruits on.

8 Cut two pieces of waxed paper to fit the base of the box. Cut a strip to go around the sides, ¼ inch (6mm) wider than the depth. Fold in this excess, trim the curves, and fit the strip inside the box. Fit one of the base shapes inside to cover the trimmed paper.

9 Arrange a layer of confectionery cups in the box, put in an assortment of fruit, and cover them with the second paper shape. Arrange another layer of paper cups and fruit on top. ✤

Note

You can vary the choice of fruit decoration according to your mood or the recipient's taste. Try making an apple orchard or a colorful fruit compote.

CHOCOLATE RUM TRUFFLES

ROLLED IN UNSWEETENED COCOA POWDER OR CHOCOLATE SPRINKLES, these rich, creamy truffles are every chocoholic's dream.

RECIPE INGREDIENTS

²/₃ cup (150ml) heavy cream

9 ounces (275g) unsweetened chocolate, broken into squares

2–3 tablespoons (30–45ml) dark rum

3–4 tablespoons chocolate sprinkles

3–4 tablespoons unsweetened cocoa powder

Makes about 24 truffles

PACKAGING NEEDS

Ruler, pencil, scissors, rubber band, craft knife, cutting mat, hole punch

Piece of medium-weight cardboard, at least 5 by 8 inches (12.5 by 20cm), for template and gift tag

Silver and colored foil

Silver-colored wire kitchen basket 6 inches (15cm) in diameter

Silver net or gauze 18 by 18 inches (45 by 45cm)

1½ yards (1.5m) silver metallic ribbon, ⅛ inch (3mm) wide

24 inches (60cm) silver metallic ribbon, ⅜ inch (8mm) wide

Tissue paper, to match the colored foil, to cover gift tag

Double-sided tape, 2 inches (5cm) wide

Silver marker pen

RECIPE: Chocolate rum truffles

1 Pour the **cream** into a heavy-bottomed saucepan and, over low heat, bring it just to a boil.

2 Remove the saucepan from the heat and, using a wooden spoon, stir in the **chocolate.** Return to the heat and stir until the chocolate melts.

3 Remove the saucepan from the heat and stir in the **rum.** Pour the mixture into a small, deep bowl and then cover. Set aside to cool for about 1 hour, then chill the mixture for at least 1 hour, or until the chocolate has set.

4 Using a melon scoop ¾ inch (2cm) in diameter, scoop out balls of the mixture and place them on a piece of waxed paper. Dip the scoop in a pitcher of warm water before you make each truffle so they come off more easily. You can also use the tip of a knife. ▶

5 Spread out the **chocolate sprinkles** on a piece of waxed paper. One at a time, roll half of the truffles in the sprinkles, lifting the corner of the paper to coat each truffle thoroughly.

6 Sift half of the **cocoa powder** onto another piece of waxed paper. Place one uncoated truffle at a time on the paper and sift some of the remaining powder over it to cover. Store the truffles in airtight containers in the refrigerator until you are ready to giftwrap them. ▪▪

GIFTWRAP: A goody basket

A silver-colored basket from the kitchenware department and glittering foil wrappers make this a gift that will shine in any company.

1 Make a 4-inch (10-cm) square template on the piece of cardboard, saving the remaining board for the gift tag. Draw around the template on the two foils. Using scissors, cut out 12 squares in each color of foil.

2 Wrap each truffle in a square of foil, folding over the edges neatly and pressing the wrapper close over the truffle. If you like, you can color-code the foil according to which type of truffle you are wrapping.

3 Pile the truffles into the basket, alternating the different-colored wrappers to best effect.

4 Place the basket in the center of the net and gather the net around the neck of the basket, beneath the handle. Use a rubber band to secure it,

5 Cut off 24 inches (60cm) of the narrow ribbon and put it together with the wider one. Use the ribbons to tie the net under the basket handle.

6 To make the gift tag, cut a rectangle 2 by 3 inches (5 by 7.5cm) from the cardboard. Cut off two corners at an angle on one short side.

7 Cut a piece of the tissue paper ¼ inch (6mm) larger all round than the cardboard. Place the board in the center of the tissue paper and fold over the edges of the paper, turning in the corners to give a neat edge.

8 Cut a piece of double-sided tape to cover the card and stick it onto the wrong side. Cut a piece of tissue paper exactly the same size as the tape. Peel off the backing strip and press the tissue paper onto it.

9 Using a hole punch, make a single hole in the shaped end of the gift tag. Write a message with the silver marker pen.

Note

Instead of using the wire container, you could package the truffles in a square of transparent paper.

10 Thread the remaining ribbon through the hole in the gift tag and loop it around the handle of the basket. Tie a neat bow to attach the tag to the parcel. 🎁

ROSE-PETAL AND ORANGE TURKISH DELIGHT

KNOWN AS *LOUKOUMI* IN GREECE AND *RAHAT LOKUM*, meaning "giving rest to the throat," in Turkey, this candy, presented in a box that hints at the contents, certainly lives up to its English name.

RECIPE: Rose-petal and orange Turkish delight

Use two pieces of thick foil to line and divide a 7-inch (18-cm) baking pan.
Fold up the central edges to create a strong partition to separate the flavors.

RECIPE INGREDIENTS

1¼ cups (300ml) water

5 envelopes (35g) unflavored gelatin

1¾ cups (375g) granulated sugar

2 tablespoons finely chopped candied
orange peel

2 teaspoons (10ml) orange juice

Orange edible food coloring

1 tablespoon roughly chopped
pistachio nuts

2 teaspoons (10ml) rosewater

Pink edible food coloring

Confectioners sugar, for dusting

PACKAGING NEEDS

*Ruler, felt-tip pen, pencil, craft knife,
cutting mat, all-purpose glue, scissors,
tracing paper, tape*

*Metal box or cardboard box covered with
aluminum foil; the metal box used here is
5"x 5"x 2" (12.5 x 12.5 x 5cm)*

*Piece of thin pink cardboard, about
4 by 8 inches (10 by 20cm)*

*Piece of thin beige cardboard, about
4 by 8 inches (10 by 20cm)*

*1 yard (1m) each pale and dark pink
sheer ribbon, 2 inches (5cm) wide*

1 Pour the **water** into a saucepan, sprinkle on the **gelatin**, and dissolve over low heat, stirring constantly with a wooden spoon. Add the **sugar** and stir until it dissolves.

2 Increase the heat and bring the mixture to a boil, then boil rapidly for 10 minutes, until the syrup is clear. Remove the saucepan from the heat and pour half the syrup into one pitcher, the other half into another pitcher.

3 Into one pitcher stir the chopped **orange peel** and **orange juice**. Add 1 or 2 drops of **orange food coloring** and stir until well blended.

4 Stir the chopped **pistachio nuts** and **rosewater** into the second pitcher of syrup and add 1 or 2 drops of **pink food coloring**. Stir until the mixture is well blended. ▶•

5 Pour the orange mixture into one half of the prepared pan and the pink mixture into the other half. Leave the candy to set in a cool place, but not the refrigerator, for 24 hours.

6 Just before you pack the candy, sift some **confectioners sugar** onto the countertop. Turn the candy out of the pan and cut it into 1-inch (2.5-cm) squares. Keeping the colors separate, sprinkle more confectioners sugar over to cover the pieces completely. ▪▪

GIFTWRAP: Squaring up

Echo the vibrant orange and pink coloring of the Turkish delight with an alternating pattern of squares glued to a metal or cardboard box.

1 If you are making a box, follow the instructions on pages 6–7. To cover this box with silver foil, follow the instructions on pages 114–15, steps 2–7, adjusting the measurements accordingly.

3 On each piece of cardboard use a pencil and ruler to draw squares the same size as those on the lid. Use a craft knife on a cutting mat to cut out the squares. You will need 24 of one color (here, pink), 21 of the other.

2 Using a ruler and felt-tip pen, measure and mark the top and sides of the lid into squares. Make sure the squares are equal in size and leave a small gap between them. Here, the squares are ¾ inch (2cm) long, with a ⅛-inch (3-mm) gap.

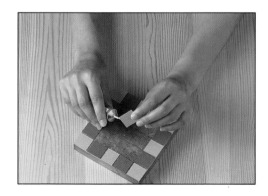

4 Glue alternate colors of cardboard onto the top of the lid, using the pen lines as a guide. Start at one corner, with a beige square, and work your way around the outside first.

5 When the top is completely covered, glue squares to the side of the lid. Remember to continue alternating the colors down the side – this is why you need more pink squares than beige ones.

6 Cut a piece of tracing paper to line the base of the box, and another to place between the layers. Pack the Turkish delight in two layers, with the colors alternating. Place the lid on the box.

7 To tie the ribbons across two opposite corners of the box, place the ribbons one on top of the other. Find the halfway mark on the ribbons and place this under one corner. Attach the ribbons to the base of the box with a strip of tape. Wind one end of the ribbons up over the next corner.

8 Continue winding the ribbons around the box. Take them under the next corner, securing with tape as before, then up on top of the box at the fourth corner. Tie a bow in the corner.

9 Adjust the bow and neatly trim the ends of the ribbons into a "V" shape with scissors.

FRENCH PISTACHIO NOUGAT

TRADITIONAL IN THE MONTELIMAR REGION OF FRANCE, this delicious candy hides crunchy nuts in its moist, colorful interior. Each piece is individually wrapped to keep its shape.

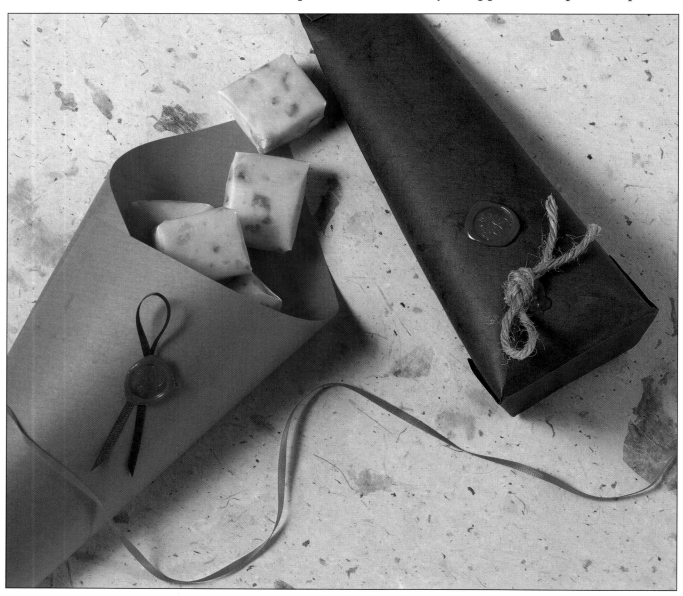

RECIPE INGREDIENTS
¼ cup (90g) honey
3 large egg whites, stiffly beaten
2 cups (375g) sugar
⅔ cup (150ml) water
3 tablespoons light corn syrup
About 2 teaspoons (10ml) rosewater
1¼ cups (150g) shelled pistachios, coarsely chopped
½ cup (90g) candied cherries, coarsely chopped
Piece of cardboard 8 by 8 inches (20 by 20cm), to put under weights (see page 72, step 5)
Transparent or waxed paper for wrapping

Makes about 1½ pounds (750g) nougat

PACKAGING NEEDS
Stapler, old knife, old teaspoon, safety matches
Piece of waxed or other stiff paper 10 by 10 inches (25 by 25cm)
Double-sided tape, ⅜ inch (8mm) wide
10 inches (25cm) soft string or double-faced satin ribbon, ⅛ inch (3mm) wide
Sealing wax
Sealing wax stamp or small coin

RECIPE: French pistachio nougat
Line a 7-inch (18-cm) square baking pan with waxed paper.

1 In a large heatproof bowl, melt the **honey** over a saucepan of simmering water. Add the **egg whites** and beat until the mixture thickens.

2 Put the **sugar, water,** and **syrup** into a saucepan. Bring to a boil and heat to 266°F (130°C) on a candy thermometer. Stir in the **rosewater.**

3 Pour the syrup into the honey mixture. Beat it, still over the saucepan of water, with a whisk for 30 to 40 minutes until it is thick, or until a little paste dropped into a cup of cold water forms a firm ball.

4 Remove the saucepan from the heat and place the bowl on the countertop. Stir in the chopped **nuts** and **cherries.** ▶

5 Pour the mixture into the lined pan and smooth the top with the back of a large spoon. Dip the spoon in hot water to stop the mixture from sticking to the spoon. Cover the surface with waxed paper, then the cardboard, and put weights or heavy cans on top to press it evenly. Leave the nougat to set firmly.

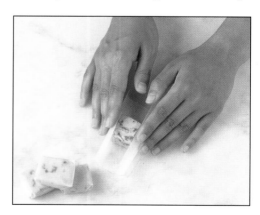

6 Mark the nougat into 1-inch (2.5-cm) squares and cut it. Immediately wrap each square in transparent or waxed paper to prevent it from drying out. ∷

GIFTWRAP: Classic cones

Elegant blue paper cones can be made in minutes to elevate simple candy into a delightful gift for any occasion.

1 Stick a piece of double-sided tape along one edge of the paper. Place the paper so that the taped edge is on your right, ready to make the cone shape.

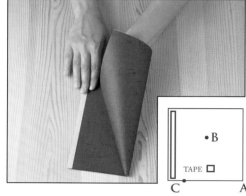

2 Take corner A (see inset) and curl it under to touch point B; point C shows where the narrow end begins. Continue curling until you have a cone; do not worry if the end is not pointed.

3 Remove the backing from the tape and stick the paper in place. At the bottom of the cone, turn a double fold to make sure that it is secured. Use double-sided tape or a staple to hold it.

4 Fill the cone with the individually wrapped nougat pieces. Do not pack in so many that the cone bulges and loses its shape.

5 Fold in about 1 inch (2.5cm) at the front of the cone.

6 Fold the flap over and crease it horizontally at the back and front. Ease up the sides and crease to make triangular shapes, as if wrapping a box. Stick the side flaps to the cone using double-sided tape. It may be useful to practice folding a piece of scrap paper first.

7 Fold the string in half and tie a knot in the center. You could also use ribbon that matches the paper.

8 Scrape off small pieces of sealing wax with the knife and put them in the old teaspoon. Heat the wax over a match flame until it melts. Immediately pour the wax in a small pool onto the point of the flap, and press on the string.

9 Melt a little more wax and pour one or more additional pools onto the cone to decorate it. Press on the seal or the coin. For a personalized gift, use a monogram seal. 🎁

Note

Try making cones in a variety of colors and give a different one to each member of the family — a cornucopia of cones. And you could also change the selection of candy to suit the recipient, or use purchased ones if you are in a hurry.

Sugar 'n' Spice Pecans

Pecan halves are candied in lightly spiced orange syrup and packed
in a preserve jar with easy-to-make embossed tin foil plaques for labels.

RECIPE INGREDIENTS

1½ cups (350g) soft light brown sugar
1 cup (250ml) orange juice
¼ cup (60g) butter
Grated rind of 1 orange
1 teaspoon mild curry powder
Large pinch ground cayenne pepper
2 cups (250g) pecan halves

The sugared nuts will fill one
1¼-pound (450-ml) jar

PACKAGING NEEDS

Soft pencil, tracing paper, scissors,
double-sided tape, all-purpose glue,
hole punch
1¼-pound (750-ml) preserving jar
8-inch (20-cm) foil baking tray, to make
the decorative label and tag
Small piece of craft paper, for gift tag
Several sheets typing paper
½ yard (45cm) silver metallic ribbon,
⅛ inch (3mm) wide
1 yard (1m) silky ribbon,
1 inch (2.5cm) wide

RECIPE: Sugar 'n' spice pecans

Line a baking tray with waxed paper, or brush it lightly with oil.

1 In a medium-sized saucepan set over low heat, stir the **sugar** and **orange juice** with a wooden spoon until the sugar has dissolved.

2 Turn up the heat, bring the syrup to a boil, and boil without stirring until it reaches 240°F (116°C) on a candy thermometer.

3 To test the temperature of the syrup without a thermometer, drop a small amount into a bowl or cup of ice water. If you can shape the sticky syrup into a soft ball that flattens when gently pressed with a finger, it is ready.

4 As soon as the syrup reaches this soft ball stage, remove the saucepan from the heat. Stir in the **butter, orange rind,** and **spices** until well-blended. Add the **pecans** and stir until they are well coated and begin to look sugary. ▶

5 Turn the mixture out of the saucepan into the prepared baking tray. Using two forks, and working quickly, pull the nuts apart to separate them.

6 Place a piece of waxed paper on a wire rack. Transfer individual nuts to the paper, using a fork, and leave them in a dry place to harden overnight. Pack them into an airtight jar until you are ready to wrap them. ◾

GIFTWRAP: Making a good impression

Present this irresistibly spicy snack in style. The labels are cut from a foil baking tray and embossed with the recipient's name.

1 Trace the design for the "pecans" label from the pattern opposite on a piece of tracing paper, using a pencil.

2 Cut two pieces from the flat part of the foil baking tray, one for the jar label, the other for the gift tag.

3 Place one piece of foil on several sheets of paper to make a soft surface. Put the "pecans" tracing on it, so that the type is reversed. With a soft, blunt pencil, go over the outlines to emboss the pattern on the foil.

4 Emboss the outline of the leaf and nut design onto the other piece of foil. Then, following the outlines of the reversed alphabet opposite, write the name of the recipient on a piece of tracing paper. With the type back to front, emboss the name in the center of the panel as before.

5 Cut out the embossed designs. Cut a piece of the silky ribbon 15 inches (38cm) long and stick the label in the middle. Wrap the ribbon around the jar, with the label at the front. Fold in the ribbon edges at the back and stick them to the glass with double-sided tape.

6 Glue the name tag to the craft paper. Cut around the tag, leaving a margin of ⅛ inch (3mm) so that the paper is just visible.

7 Punch a hole at one end of the name tag and loop the metallic ribbon through it.

8 Coil the remaining silky ribbon inside the jar and arrange the pecans between the folds.

9 Thread the metallic ribbon through the fastening on the jar and tie on the gift tag. 🎁

SUGAR-PASTE LEAVES

DECORATE A TERRA-COTTA POT with trailing ivy and fill it with multicolored
edible leaves for an attractive and down-to-earth gift.

RECIPE INGREDIENTS

1¼ cups (250g) granulated sugar

⅓ cup (75ml) water

1 teaspoon cream of tartar

Orange, yellow, and green edible food colorings

Orange, vanilla, and peppermint extracts

Confectioners sugar, sifted, for dusting

Small leaf-shaped confectionery or cookie cutters

Makes 8 ounces (250g) leaves

PACKAGING NEEDS

Pencil, tracing paper, craft knife, cutting mat, masking tape, scissors, scrap of cardboard, rubber band

Stencil with trailing leaf design (page 80)

Earthenware flowerpot, about 4 inches (10cm) in diameter

Green and brown dry-brush stencil paints

Stencil brush

Piece of cellophane 8 by 8 inches (20 by 20cm)

Cotton table napkin, about 20 by 20 inches (50 by 50cm)

1 yard (1m) wire-edged ribbon, 3 inches (7.5cm) wide, in a contrasting color

RECIPE: Sugar-paste leaves

1 Put the **sugar** and **water** into a saucepan and dissolve over low heat, stirring with a long-handled metal spoon. Bring the syrup to a boil and stir in the **cream of tartar**. Boil without stirring until the syrup registers 240°F (116°C) on a candy thermometer.

3 Using a spatula, "knead" the sugar paste by turning it over, forward and backward, in a figure-eight movement. When the paste is opaque, gather it into a ball and knead it until it is smooth. Set it aside to cool completely.

2 Brush a little cold water over a large cold surface, such as a marble slab or chopping board, and pour on the syrup. Let it cool for about 3 to 5 minutes until a skin begins to form around the edges.

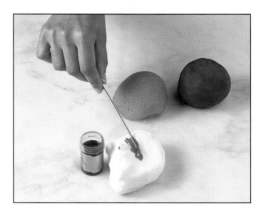

4 Divide the paste into three. Using a skewer, color each one with 2 to 3 drops of **food coloring** and add the appropriate **extract**. Knead each portion until the coloring and flavoring are well blended. ▶

5 Dust the countertop very lightly with sifted **confectioners sugar** and roll out each portion of paste to a thickness of ¼ inch (6mm). Cut out leaf shapes, using small confectionery or cookie cutters. Gather up the trimmings in each separate color, roll them out again, and cut out more shapes.

6 Using a sharp knife, mark lines on the shapes to represent leaf veins. Arrange the finished leaves in a single layer on a wire rack and leave them in a warm place to dry overnight. ▪▪

GIFTWRAP: Gathering the harvest

Create a combined gift for the kitchen window sill and breakfast table by enclosing an earthenware pot of edible leaves in a two-tone cotton table napkin.

1 Draw around the outline of the stencil below on tracing paper and use a craft knife to cut it out. Attach masking tape to the stencil and position it on the pot so that the leaf pattern winds around it.

2 Mix the two colors of dry-brush paint on the scrap of cardboard to make varying shades. Then, working with one color at a time, stencil the leaf design on the pot.

3 Reposition the stencil so that the leaves continue to wind around the pot. Continue stenciling the outline, then set the pot aside and let the paint dry thoroughly.

4 To prevent the sugar-paste leaves from touching the inside of the flowerpot, push the square of cellophane into the pot.

5 Fill the pot with the edible leaves. Draw the corners of the cellophane over the top.

6 Place the napkin right side down on the work surface, stand the flowerpot in the center, and bring the four corners over the top to enclose the pot. Secure with a rubber band.

7 Tie the ribbon around the rubber band to hide it and make a bow. Trim the ribbon ends neatly with a pair of scissors. 🎁

Note

In place of a flowerpot, you could pack the sugar-paste leaves into an airtight container or mason jar before wrapping it in a cotton table napkin. For an even simpler gift, you could omit the wrapping altogether and decorate the container with a dried seed pod, as here.

SUGAR-FROSTED FRUITS

FIRM, JUST-RIPE FRUIT with contrasting colors, flavors, and textures
are presented in a decorative giant matchbox.

RECIPE: Sugar-frosted fruits

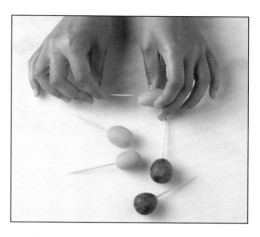

RECIPE INGREDIENTS

*About 12 ounces (375g) mixed fresh fruit,
such as kumquats, grapes, cherries,
raspberries, blackberries, red currants, Cape
gooseberries, and small strawberries*

1 large egg white

½ cup (90g) superfine sugar

*Toothpicks or skewers, to hold
stemless fruits*

Frosts about 12 ounces (375g)
small fruit

PACKAGING NEEDS

*Ruler, pencil, craft knife, cutting mat,
scissors, double-sided tape*

*Piece of medium-weight cardboard 6¾ by
11⅝ inches (17.3 by 29.8cm), for the box*

*Piece of thin cardboard 7⅞ by 12¼ inches
(20 by 31cm), for the wraparound slide*

*Piece of wrapping paper 9⅜ by 12¼ inches
(24 by 31cm), to cover the slide*

Small confectionery fluted cups

*About ¾ yard (70cm) wire-edged ribbon,
2 inches (5cm) wide*

1 Rinse the **fruit** under cold running water, taking care not to bruise them. Keep the stems on if possible for more attractive presentation, and retain the papery Cape gooseberry cases, if used. Dry the fruit gently on paper towel.

2 Using a toothpick or fine skewer, carefully pierce each piece of fruit that does not have a stem.

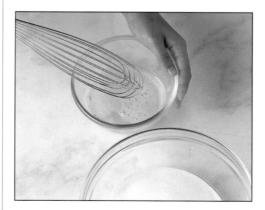

3 In a small bowl, lightly beat the **egg white** using a wire whisk. Place the **sugar** in a larger bowl.

4 One by one, dip the pieces of fruit in the egg white to coat them and shake off the excess. Hold the fruit with the toothpick or stem, as applicable. ▶

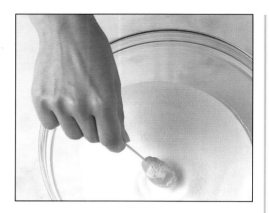

5 Dip the egg-white coated fruit in the sugar, turning it to cover the fruit completely. Use a teaspoon, if necessary, to sprinkle sugar over any parts that remain uncovered.

6 Place the fruit on a wire rack in a warm, dry place, such as on top of a low stove, and leave to dry for several hours or overnight. When dry, carefully remove the toothpicks. ▪

GIFTWRAP: A fruitful package

An outsize matchbox covered in bright giftwrap, this sliding box can be used to present many other sweet things, too. (See page 126 for templates of box and sliding cover.)

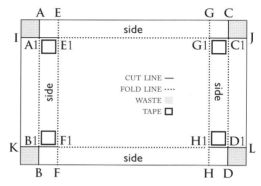

1 To make the box, use the medium-weight cardboard. Follow the pattern and use a craft knife to score (not cut) lines A-B and C-D, each ¾ inch (2cm) in from and parallel to the short sides. Then score lines E-F and G-H, each 1⅛ inch (2.9cm) in from and parallel to those lines. Score lines I-J and K-L, each 1⅛ inch (2.9cm) in from and parallel to the long sides.

2 Using a craft knife, cut away the rectangles at the four corners, and cut through the lines A1-E1, C1-G1, D1-H1, and B1-F1. Stick 1-inch (2.5-cm) squares of double-sided tape where indicated by the bold outlines on the pattern.

3 Peel the backing strips from the tape, fold up the long sides of the box, and press the corner flaps to the tape. Fold over the two narrow end sections, I-A1-B1-K and J-C1-D1-L.

4 To make the wraparound slide, score a line ½ inch (1.5cm) from and parallel to one of the short sides of the thinner card. Then score another line a further 1¼ inches (3cm) along, another a further 4⅝ inches (11.75cm) and another a further 1¼ inches (3cm) along. This last line will be 4⅝ inches (11.75cm) in from the opposite edge.

5 Cover the entire back of the wrapping paper from edge to edge with strips of double-sided tape and trim the ends, using the craft knife.

6 With the double-sided tape up, measure and mark a spot ¾ inch (2cm) in from each of the long edges at both ends. Peel off the backing strips and, using the marked spots as a guide, place the cardboard, scored side up, so that the short edges of the cardboard and paper align.

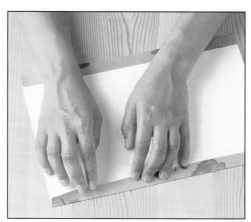

7 Press the cardboard down firmly onto the wrapping paper and fold the excess paper over the cardboard.

8 Bend the cardboard along the scored lines and secure the overlap with double-sided tape or glue.

9 Arrange the confectionery cups in the box and put a piece of frosted fruit in each one. Slide the cover over the box and tie the ribbon into a bow around it. Trim the ribbon ends neatly. ✿

Cakes & Desserts

🎁 A CAKE CAN MAKE AN OCCASION.
Express the spirit of the holiday
season with Thanksgiving pumpkin
pie or rich Christmas fruitcake baked
in a round mold. For Valentine's day,
offer frosted rose-petal cake, light-
as-air cake, or four-layer spice cake
with a sugar and cinnamon bow.
Old-fashioned gingerbread is given a
lift with edible gold leaf; cocoa and
candied fruits light up an Italian
fruitcake; and no one will be able to
resist chocolate-pecan gateau or
butterscotch-topped cheesecake.

Ready-made boxes are featured here:
painted with a crackle finish, adorned
with pressed leaves, and covered with
floral paper. A wooden sieve and an
open-weave basket are also pressed
into service. Candy wrappers brighten
tissue paper, and flamboyant bows
are the accent on a homemade box
and a simple fabric package. And
presenting your dessert on a beautiful
plate will save your hostess time and
be a lasting gift.

ROSE-PETAL CAKE

FLAVORED WITH ROSEWATER AND SCENTED ROSE PETALS and decorated with sugar-frosted petals, this cake sets the scene for an elegant and romantic rendezvous.

RECIPE INGREDIENTS

½ cup (125g) butter, at room temperature

½ cup plus 2 tablespoons (125g) superfine sugar

2 large eggs, separated

1 cup (125g) unsifted all-purpose flour

1 tablespoon (15ml) rosewater

About 12 fragrant rose petals, rinsed and patted dry

FROSTING

1-2 teaspoons (5-10ml) rosewater

½ cup (125g) confectioners sugar, sifted

Makes one 7-inch (18-cm) cake

PACKAGING NEEDS

Hairdryer, waxed paper, all-purpose glue, scissors

Round wooden, cardboard, or papier-mâché box and lid 8 inches (20cm) in diameter and at least 3½ inches (9cm) deep

Vinyl matte water-based paints in two contrasting shades of pink

½-inch (1.5-cm) paintbrush

Clear water-based satin varnish

Small piece of sponge

3 small containers, such as foil muffin cups

Tissue paper

DECORATION FOR CAKE AND BOX

2 large egg whites, lightly beaten

3 heaping tablespoons superfine sugar

Individual rose petals, rinsed and patted dry, for the cake

2 or 3 pink rosebuds, slightly open, for the box

24 inches (60cm) gossamer ribbon, 1½ inches (4cm) wide

RECIPE: Rose-petal cake

Preheat the oven to 350°F (180°C). Lightly brush a 7-inch (18-cm) cake pan with oil or melted butter and dust it with flour, tipping out any excess flour.

1 In a mixing bowl, cream the **butter** and **sugar** together until they are light and fluffy, then beat in the **egg yolks** a little at a time.

2 In another bowl, beat the egg whites until stiff. Lightly fold them and the **flour** alternately into the butter mixture. Stir in the **rosewater.**

3 Line the bottom of the prepared cake pan with the **rose petals** and pour in the batter. (The petals impart a delicate rose flavor to the cake, but do not retain their color when baked.)

4 Bake in the preheated oven for about 35 minutes, until the cake is lightly brown and feels springy to the touch. Leave the cake to cool in the pan for a few minutes before turning it out onto a wire rack to cool completely. ▶

5 To make the frosting, stir just enough **rosewater** into the **confectioners sugar** to give a coating consistency. Spread it over the top and side of the cake using a metal spatula.

6 To make the frosted rose petals for decoration, see steps 6 and 7 on page 91. Arrange the rose petals on the cake, using a little more frosting to attach them if the cake frosting has already set. ▪▪

GIFTWRAP: Summer flowers

A papier-mâché box with a scalloped lid, painted in two shades of pink and trimmed with sugar-frosted roses, is as decorative as the cake it holds.

1 Pour a little of the darker pink paint into one of the containers and paint the base and sides of the box, brushing the paint on in one direction only. Wash the paintbrush.

2 Pour a little of the varnish into a container and, working quickly, while the pink paint is still wet, brush on the varnish.

3 Dry with the hairdryer until the varnish crackles, then leave the container to dry completely.

4 Pour a little of the contrasting paint into another container and make a pad with the sponge. Dip the sponge into the paint and rub it into the cracks all over the box.

5 Paint the lid in a similar way, but brush it first with the paler color. While this is wet, apply the varnish, "crackle" with the hairdryer, and when it is totally dry, rub in the darker color.

6 To make the decoration for the cake and the box, put the lightly beaten **egg whites** in a shallow bowl and the **sugar** on a plate. One at a time, brush the **petals** and **rosebuds** with the egg, covering every surface. Allow any excess to drip back into the bowl.

7 Using a teaspoon, sprinkle the superfine sugar over the petals and buds, making sure to cover all the surfaces. Place them on a sheet of waxed paper to dry and leave them in a warm place for at least 3 hours.

8 When they are dry, tie the frosted roses into a bunch with the ribbon and glue them to the lid of the box. Trim the ribbon ends neatly with scissors.

9 Line the box with the tissue paper before putting in the cake. Carefully lower it into the box using a strip of waxed paper (for tips on how to do this, see page 95, step 9). ✤

Note

You can frost the rose petals or rosebuds well in advance of making the cake. Once they are thoroughly dry, store them between layers of paper towel in an airtight container.

CHOCOLATE-PECAN GATEAU

MADE WITH GROUND PECANS AND WITHOUT ANY FLOUR, this rich, sumptuous cake has a glossy chocolate topping, decorated with chocolate-coated nuts.

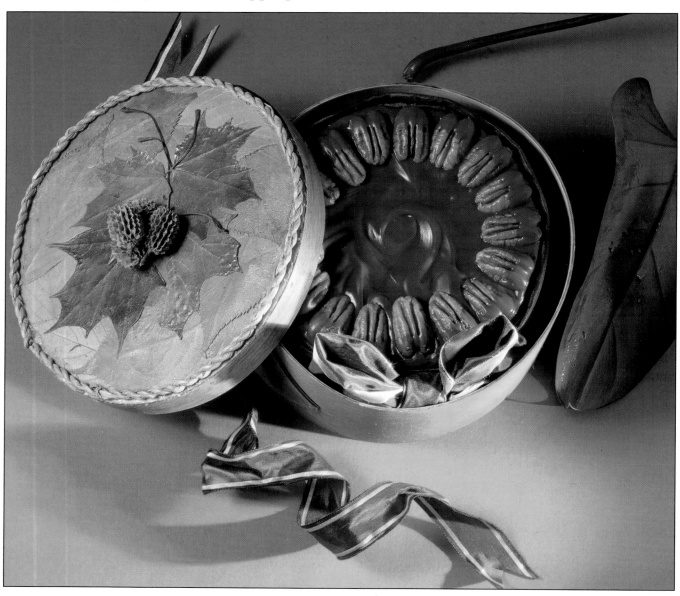

RECIPE INGREDIENTS

6 ounces (175g) semisweet chocolate

6 tablespoons (90g) butter

⅓ cup (60g) superfine sugar

3 large eggs

1 teaspoon (5ml) vanilla extract

1½ cups (90g) large pecans, ground

About 20 pecan halves

FROSTING

2 tablespoons (30ml) clear honey

3 tablespoons (45g) butter

3 ounces (90g) semisweet chocolate

Makes one 6-inch (15-cm) cake

PACKAGING NEEDS

Clear furniture polish, soft polishing cloth, all-purpose glue, scissors, waxed paper, double-sided tape

Wooden or cardboard box with lid, at least 6½ inches (16.5cm) in diameter and 3 inches (7.5cm) deep

Medium-brown wood stain

¾-inch (2-cm) paintbrush

Selection of golden fallen leaves, pressed (see Note page 95)

Thick string, at least 21 inches (53.5cm) long

Matte polyurethane varnish

3 to 6 small pine cones

¾ yard (70cm) silk ribbon, 2½ inches (6.5cm) wide

RECIPE: Chocolate-pecan gateau

Preheat the oven to 350°F (180°C). Line a 6-inch (15-cm) round cake pan with waxed paper.

1 Place the **chocolate,** broken in pieces, and **butter** in a saucepan over low heat. Stir occasionally until the mixture has melted, then remove it from the heat and let it cool slightly.

2 Beat the **sugar, eggs,** and **vanilla extract,** preferably with an electric mixer, until the mixture is pale and creamy. Using a metal spoon, fold in the chocolate mixture and ground **nuts** until the batter is well blended.

3 Pour the batter into the prepared pan and smooth the top. Bake in the preheated oven for 30 to 35 minutes, until the cake feels springy to the touch. Stand the pan on a wire rack to cool. Turn the cake out when cool.

4 To make the frosting, melt the **honey, butter,** and **chocolate** in a small bowl set over a saucepan of simmering water, stirring occasionally. ▶

5 Lift the bowl off the saucepan and dip the pecan halves into the mixture to half-coat them. Place the nuts on waxed paper to dry.

6 Turn the cake upside-down and remove the paper. Spread the frosting over the top of the cake only, using a spatula dipped in hot water. Arrange the nuts around the edge. Store the cake in an airtight container once the frosting sets. ▪▪

GIFTWRAP: A patchwork of leaves

A wooden box covered with a patchwork of golden leaves, this is a perfect package to take to your host at Thanksgiving.

1 Following directions on the product, brush stain evenly over the side and base of the box and the side of the lid. Let dry and apply another coat if you wish.

2 When the stain is dry, rub the treated areas with furniture polish.

3 Spread a thin coat of glue over the outer edge of the box lid. Arrange pressed leaves around the rim, spreading glue thinly over leaves where they overlap.

4 With the scissors, carefully cut close to the edge of the lid, trimming off the parts of any leaves that hang over the edge of the rim.

5 Complete the patchwork of leaves, then glue the string around the outside edge of the lid to protect the cut edges of the leaves. Brush the leaves with varnish and set aside to dry.

6 Arrange a cluster of cones in the center of the lid to see how they look. When you are happy with the combination, glue them in place.

7 Cut a 20- by 2½-inch (50- by 6.5-cm) strip of waxed paper. Wrap the band around the cake and seal the seam with double-sided tape.

8 Cut off a 20-inch (50-cm) length of ribbon and turn under the two edges to hide them. Stick a strip of double-sided tape vertically down the paper band. Wrap the ribbon around the cake and stick down the ends. Tie a small bow with the remaining ribbon and attach it to the band with tape to cover the seam.

9 Line the box with a circle of waxed paper. Place the cake on a strip of waxed paper and gently lower it into the box. Carefully slide the paper out from under the cake. ✽

Note

Gather a selection of leaves to press in the fall, since their colors come up well when dried. Dust the leaves and pat off any dampness with paper towels. Arrange them in a single layer between sheets of paper and place them in a large book such as a telephone directory, and put more books or weights on top. The leaves should be dry and pressed flat in two to three weeks.

OLD-FASHIONED GINGERBREAD

UNWRAP THE GIANT CANDY TO REVEAL A MOIST GINGERBREAD, full of candied ginger and topped with edible gold leaf, which keeps well and even improves with time.

RECIPE INGREDIENTS

1½ cups (175g) unsifted all-purpose flour

2 teaspoons ground ginger

½ teaspoon ground cinnamon

¼ teaspoon grated nutmeg

Pinch salt

½ cup (90g) finely chopped candied ginger

⅓ cup (80ml) dark molasses

¼ cup (60g) butter

½ cup (100g) firmly packed soft dark brown sugar

1 large egg, lightly beaten

3 tablespoons (45ml) milk

½ teaspoon baking soda

DECORATION

2 tablespoons (30ml) honey

Edible gold leaf

Makes one 1-pound (500-g) cake

PACKAGING NEEDS

Foil, waxed paper, scissors, tape, paper glue

1 sheet tissue paper

New 1-pound (500-g) loaf pan

Foil candy wrappers, or pieces of gold, silver, and colored foil wrapping

Double-sided tape, ⅜ inch (8mm) wide

½ yard (45cm) each of 2 colors of satin ribbon, ⅛ inch (3mm) wide

RECIPE: Old-fashioned gingerbread

Preheat the oven to 350°F (180°C). Line a 1-pound (500-g) loaf pan with waxed paper.

1 Sift the **flour**, **spices**, and **salt** into a mixing bowl. Stir in the chopped **ginger**. In a small saucepan, over low heat, melt the **molasses**, **butter**, and **sugar** stirring occasionally.

2 Gradually pour the melted sugar mixture into the dry ingredients and stir well with a wooden spoon. Beat in the **egg**.

3 Put the **milk** into a cup and sprinkle the **baking soda** onto it. Stir well and then stir it into the mixture in the bowl.

4 Pour the batter into the prepared pan and smooth the top. Bake in the preheated oven for 40 to 45 minutes. To test if baked through, insert a skewer into the middle; it should come out clean. ▶

5 Stand the pan on a wire rack and leave the gingerbread to cool slightly before turning it out. Melt the **honey** and brush it over the top of the cake while it is still warm.

6 Tear off small pieces of **gold leaf** and press them onto the cake, using a small craft brush. When the cake is cool, wrap it tightly in foil and store it an airtight container until you are ready to wrap it. ▪▪

GIFTWRAP: A gingerbread cracker

Give a sparkling new baking pan as part of the gift – particularly apt for a keen cook – so the recipient can make the gingerbread again and again.

1 If necessary, remove the old foil from the cake and rewrap the gingerbread tightly in a fresh piece of foil.

2 Overwrap the cake in waxed paper, sticking down the edges neatly with tape.

3 Carefully place the wrapped cake in the new loaf pan. The wrapping may create a snug fit.

4 Prepare the candy wrappers or pieces of foil wrapping by gently smoothing out the foil, using your thumbnail.

5 With the tissue paper right side up on the work surface, place the pan in the center of the paper and place a string or ribbon around the outside of it. Then glue candy wrappers or scraps of colored foil around the outside of the ribbon, using dabs of glue.

6 Continue sticking on candy wrappers, placing them at random to give a patchwork effect. You will need to glue all around the outline, so that the sides and top of the pan are covered when it is wrapped.

7 Place the tissue paper right side down on the work surface. Position the cake pan in the center of the paper, checking to see that it sits on the undecorated area. Fold over the long sides of the paper to make a neat edge.

8 Bring the long sides of the paper up over the pan and make a pleated fold so that the candy wrappers meet in the middle and overlap slightly. Use some double-sided tape to secure the package.

9 To make the ends of the package, carefully pinch in the tissue paper, taking care not to tear it. Cut the ribbons in half. Tie them around each end of the package, forming a bow. Trim the ends of the tissue paper and open them out. 🎁

Note

For a simpler look, or if you are pressed for time, you may prefer to wrap the gingerbread in its pan in undecorated tissue paper. Tie the two ribbons crosswise around the package. Alternatively, you could add a flamboyant ready-made bow.

BUTTERSCOTCH-TOPPED CHEESECAKE

THE ATTRACTIVE PRESENTATION OF THIS CHEESECAKE on a decorative plate, not to mention the buttery smooth taste, makes it an ideal gift for a dinner party.

RECIPE INGREDIENTS

CRUST
5 tablespoons (75g) lightly salted butter

1 cup (125g) crushed gingersnap crumbs

FILLING
2 tablespoons seedless raisins

2 tablespoons (30ml) sweet sherry or brandy

12 ounces (375g) cream cheese

2 large eggs

½ cup plus 2 tablespoons (125g)
superfine sugar

¼ cup (30g) unsifted all-purpose flour

⅔ cup (150ml) sour cream

Grated rind of 1 orange

2 tablespoons (30ml) orange juice

BUTTERSCOTCH TOPPING
¾ cup (180ml) sweetened condensed milk

¼ cup plus 2 tablespoons (60g)
superfine sugar

6 tablespoons (90g) butter

2 tablespoons (30ml) honey

PACKAGING NEEDS
Tape, scissors, rubber band

Strip of waxed paper, about
2½ by 25 inches (6.5 by 63cm)

About 30 inches (76cm) grosgrain ribbon,
1 inch (2.5cm) wide

About 25 dried bay leaves

About 13 kumquats

Dinner plate or serving plate with an
8-inch (20-cm) flat center

Clear cellophane, about 1 yard
(1m) square

6 inches (15cm) satin ribbon,
3 inches (7.5cm) wide

10 inches (25cm) medium-gauge
flexible wire

Toothpick

RECIPE: Butterscotch-topped cheesecake

Preheat the oven to 350°F (180°C). Lightly brush an 8-inch (20-cm) springform cake pan with vegetable oil.

1 Melt the **butter** in a small saucepan, then stir in the **gingersnap** crumbs. Turn the mixture into the cake pan and press it with the back of a spoon to cover the bottom. Set aside while you make the filling.

2 Soak the **raisins** in the **sherry** and set aside. Using a wire whisk, beat together the **cream cheese** and **eggs** in a mixing bowl, then beat in the **sugar**.

3 Fold in the **flour** and the **sour cream** with a metal spoon. Stir in the raisins and any sherry, the **orange rind** and **orange juice**.

4 Pour the batter into the pan, smooth the top, and bake in the preheated oven for 45 minutes, or until a skewer inserted into the center comes out clean. Stand on a wire rack to cool completely. ▶

5 For the topping, put the **condensed milk, sugar, butter,** and **honey** into a saucepan and stir over low heat until they melt. Bring to a boil, and boil for 3 minutes without stirring.

6 Immediately pour the butterscotch mixture over the cheesecake and set it aside to cool. Wrap the cheesecake, still in the pan, in foil and store it in the refrigerator until you are ready to giftwrap it. ▪

GIFTWRAP: Presentation plate

You might like to get together with other guests going to a party and take your buffet gifts on a set of matching plates.

1 Remove the cheesecake from the cake pan, wrap the waxed paper strip around the side, and join the edges with tape.

2 Cut 25 inches (63cm) of the grosgrain ribbon and wrap it around the cheesecake. Tape the seam; if you wish, you can add a bow to hide it.

3 Arrange the bay leaves around the cheesecake, between the paper and the ribbon band. Place a kumquat in the center and add two more bay leaves.

4 Place the plate in the center of the square of cellophane. Using a metal spatula, place the cheesecake in the center of the plate.

5 Draw the corners of the paper over the top of the cheesecake and use a rubber band to hold them in place.

6 Tie the piece of wide satin ribbon over the rubber band to hide it. Tuck in the ends of the ribbon so they do not show.

7 Thread the kumquats onto the medium-gauge wire. It may help if you make a hole with a toothpick in each fruit first so that you can arrange them neatly on the wire.

8 Wrap the kumquat-covered wire around the top of the package, just below the ribbon, and twist the ends of the wire to secure the ring. If necessary, trim off any extra wire.

9 Once the kumquat ring is in place, arrange the cellophane by pulling out the top of the package with your fingers. ❖

Note

If you present the cheesecake on a less decorative plate and do not have far to travel, you could omit the wrapping in cellophane and make a larger kumquat ring to form a border around the dessert.

ITALIAN CHOCOLATE FRUITCAKE

COMBINING NUTS, CANDIED FRUITS, AND COCOA, this chewy Italian panforte
has something to appeal to all palates.

RECIPE INGREDIENTS

*1 cup (125g) chopped blanched almonds,
plus 4 whole ones for decoration*

1 cup (125g) chopped hazelnuts

½ cup (60g) chopped pecan halves

⅓ cup (60g) chopped dried figs

*1⅓ cups (250g) chopped mixed candied
fruits, such as pineapple, apricots,
lemon, and pears*

½ cup (60g) unsifted all-purpose flour

*5 tablespoons unsweetened cocoa
powder, sifted*

*1 teaspoon ground cinnamon, plus extra
for dusting*

¼ teaspoon ground cloves

*½ cup plus 2 tablespoons (125g)
granulated sugar*

⅓ cup (80ml) honey

1 teaspoon (5ml) rosewater

*2 tablespoons confectioners sugar, sifted,
for dusting*

Makes one 8-inch (20-cm) cake

PACKAGING NEEDS

*Scissors, masking tape, rubber gloves, ruler,
pencil, rubber band*

*A shallow woven basket with a handle,
at least 8½ by 8½ inches (21.5 by 21.5cm)*

*Mauve and pink latex or acrylic
water-based paints*

2 small containers, such as foil muffin cups

Medium-grade steel wool

½-inch (1.5-cm) paintbrush

Sheet of parchment paper

Calligraphy pen and ink

*1 yard (1m) cotton ribbon,
½ inch (1.5cm) wide*

Tissue paper, to line basket

RECIPE: Italian chocolate fruitcake

*Preheat the oven to 350°F (180°C). Line the bottom and sides of an 8-inch (20-cm)
square baking pan with waxed paper.*

1 Spread the chopped **almonds** and **hazelnuts** on a baking tray and toast them in the preheated oven for 5 to 6 minutes, stirring them once or twice, until they are brown. Leave them to cool slightly.

2 In a mixing bowl, stir together the toasted chopped almonds and hazelnuts, the **pecans**, and the chopped **figs** and other **fruits**.

3 Sift in the **flour, cocoa powder, cinnamon,** and **cloves** and stir the ingredients well.

4 Heat the **sugar** and **honey** in a saucepan over low heat until the sugar melts. Pour the syrup into the dry ingredients, add the **rosewater**, and mix well. ▶

5 Spoon the mixture into the prepared pan and press it into the corners with a wooden spoon. Bake in the preheated oven for 35 to 40 minutes, until a skewer inserted in the center of the cake comes out clean.

6 Stand the pan on a wire rack to cool, then turn out the cake and peel off the paper. Sift **confectioners sugar** over the top and decorate it with whole toasted almonds. (To store the cake, wrap it in foil and place it in an airtight container without dusting it with confectioners sugar.) ▦

GIFTWRAP: Carrying on the tradition

Presenting your gift with a scroll containing a handwritten copy of this centuries-old recipe will mean that it can be enjoyed for a long time to come.

1 Cut strips of masking tape and stick it around the rim of the basket and over the handle to protect these areas while you apply the mauve paint to the rest of the basket.

2 Pour a little of the mauve paint into a foil container. Put on the rubber gloves and tear off a piece of steel wool about 2 inches (5cm) square. Crumple it to make a workable pad.

3 Dip the pad into the paint and rub it onto the basket, working in the direction of the grain on each of the wood strips. Do not try to paint right into the edges of the squares; it makes a more interesting checked effect if you do not.

4 When the paint is dry, peel off the masking tape from the rim and handle. Apply more tape around the top of the basket, just beneath the rim, to protect the painted area.

5 Pour a little of the pink paint into the second container. Using the brush, paint the rim and both sides of the handle. Leave the paint to dry, then peel off the tape.

6 Measure and cut a piece of the parchment paper about 8 by 10 inches (20 by 25cm), or to suit the size of your handwriting. Copy the recipe for the fruit cake, using a calligraphy pen and ink.

7 Cut off 24 inches (60cm) of the ribbon. To make a scroll, roll up the recipe, secure it with a rubber band, and tie the ribbon around it. Remove the band after the ribbon is tied into a bow.

8 To make a gift tag, cut a small piece of the parchment paper, write a message on it, roll it up, and tie it to the handle of the basket with the remaining ribbon.

9 Place the tissue paper in the basket to line it and carefully put the cake on top of the paper. Trim the tissue paper with scissors and tuck in the edges so that they do not stick above the rim. Balance the recipe scroll across one corner of the basket. ✼

Note

On the recipe scroll, you could include hints on how to serve the cake. Traditionally, it is cut into thin rectangular pieces and enjoyed with a cup of strong Italian coffee or a sweet fortified wine, such as Vin Santo.

FOUR-LAYER SPICE CAKE

THIS "ANYTIME" CAKE, WITH ITS SUGAR AND CINNAMON BOW, can be served
with a cup of coffee or tea, or as a dessert.

RECIPE INGREDIENTS

½ cup (125g) lightly salted butter, softened

¾ cup plus 2 tablespoons (175g) granulated sugar

½ cup (125g) soft dark brown sugar, packed

3 large eggs

½ cup (125ml) milk

⅓ cup (80ml) molasses

2⅓ cups unsifted all-purpose (300g) flour

1 teaspoon salt

½ teaspoon baking soda

2 teaspoons ground cinnamon

¼ teaspoon each ground cloves and nutmeg

FROSTING AND DECORATION

½ cup (125g) lightly salted butter

⅓ cup (80ml) molasses

3 tablespoons (45ml) milk

1¾–2 cups (175–250g) confectioners sugar

2 tablespoons superfine sugar

1 teaspoon ground cinnamon

Bow-shaped stencil outline (page 127), plus thin cardboard 8 by 8 inches (20 by 20cm)

Makes one 6-inch (15-cm) cake

PACKAGING NEEDS

Ruler, soft pencil, craft knife, cutting mat, tape, double-sided tape, tracing paper

Wooden strainer 7 inches (18cm) in diameter, or a cardboard box 3 inches (7.5cm) deep

Piece of heavy cardboard 7½ by 7½ inches (19 by 19cm), for the lid

Piece of thin cardboard 2 by 24 inches (5 by 61cm), for the side of the lid

Piece of craft paper 10½ by 24 inches (26 by 61cm), to cover the lid

Latex or acrylic water-based paint

Small craft paintbrush

Gold craft powder

About 1¾ yards (1.6m) ribbon, 2½ inches (6.5cm) wide

RECIPE: Four-layer spice cake

Preheat the oven to 350°F (180°C). Lightly brush two 6-inch (15-cm) cake pans with oil and dust them with flour, shaking out the excess.

1 In a mixing bowl, cream the **butter** with a wooden spoon. Gradually beat in the **granulated** and **dark brown sugars** and beat until light and fluffy. Beat in the **eggs** one at a time.

2 Gradually beat in the **milk** and **molasses**. Sift together the **flour, salt, baking soda, cinnamon, cloves,** and **nutmeg**, then gradually add the dry ingredients to the butter mixture. Beat until well blended.

3 Pour the batter into the prepared pans, smooth the tops, and bake in the preheated oven for 40 to 45 minutes, until a skewer inserted into the middle comes out clean. Cool the cakes in the pans, then turn them out onto a wire rack to cool completely.

4 To make the frosting, melt the **butter** and **molasses** in a saucepan over low heat. Stir in the **milk,** and mix well. Let the mixture cool, then sift in enough **confectioners sugar** to make a thick, spreadable consistency. ▶

5 While the frosting cools, cut each of the cake layers in half horizontally. Spread three of them with the frosting using a spatula dipped in hot water, and sandwich them together.

6 Sift together the **superfine sugar** and the remaining ground cinnamon. Place the bow-shaped stencil (see steps 6 and 7 opposite) on top of the cake and sift the spiced sugar over it. Carefully lift off the stencil, to preserve the crisp outlines of the decoration. ▪▪

GIFTWRAP: Tied up in bows

The cake is presented in a surprise gift box – a wooden strainer with a simple-to-make cardboard lid – decorated, like the cake itself, with a ribbon bow motif.

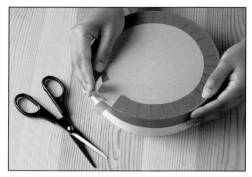

1 Make the lid following the general instructions to make the round box lid on pages 8–9.

3 Position the lid on the paper with the top ½ inch (1.5cm) from one side and the inside ¼ inch (6mm) from the other. Peel off the backing and press the strip firmly around the side of the lid, smoothing it as you go.

2 To cover the lid, measure the circumference of the lid and the depth plus ¾ inch (2cm). Cut a strip of craft paper this size. Here, the strip is 24 inches (61cm) long and 2¾ inches (7cm) wide. Cover the paper strip on the wrong side with double-sided tape.

4 Snip the paper at intervals around the overlapping edges to make folding easier. Fold over the two edges and press them firmly in place on the inside and the top of the lid.

5 Cut a circle of the craft paper to fit the top of the lid exactly. Cover the paper on the wrong side with strips of double-sided tape and trim the edges.

6 Trace the ribbon-and-bow outline on page 127 onto the tracing paper. Place the paper on a piece of cardboard and press hard over the design with a soft pencil.

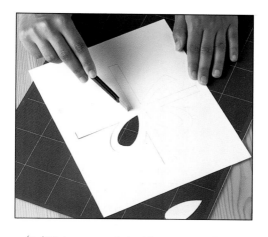

7 Using a craft knife on a cutting mat, cut out the bow shape from the cardboard. This will also be used as a stencil to make the "ribbon" on the cake.

8 Place the bow-shaped stencil outline in the center of the paper circle and draw around the shape with a pencil. Paint in the ribbon-and-bow shape. If the paper you choose is absorbent, you might need to go over the shape a second time.

9 Peel off the backing strips from the double-sided tape and stick the paper circle to the lid. Brush the painted motif lightly with the gold craft powder.

10 Carefully lower the cake into the strainer (see page 95, step 9), taking care not to damage the sugar bow. Carefully tuck in about 16 inches (40cm) of the ribbon around the cake, between the cake and the strainer. Put the lid on the strainer. Wrap the remaining ribbon around the package and tie a bow. Trim the ends neatly. 🎁

THANKSGIVING PUMPKIN PIE

PUMPKIN AND PECANS COMBINE TO MAKE A RICH, CRUNCHY PIE
that is the perfect contribution to a festive meal.

RECIPE INGREDIENTS

1½ cups (175g) unsifted all-purpose flour

2 teaspoons superfine sugar

½ teaspoon salt

2 teaspoons grated orange rind

6 tablespoons (90g) cold unsalted butter

1 large egg yolk

3 tablespoons (45ml) heavy cream

FILLING

3 cups (500g) pumpkin, peeled, seeded and cubed (prepared weight) or 2 cups pureed canned pumpkin

2 large eggs, lightly beaten

½ cup (90g) packed light brown sugar

2 teaspoons ground cinnamon

1 teaspoon ground ginger

½ teaspoon salt

3 tablespoons (45ml) molasses

¼ cup (60ml) heavy cream

2 tablespoons (30ml) orange juice

1 cup (125g) pecan halves

Milk, for brushing

Confectioners sugar, sifted, for dusting

PACKAGING NEEDS

Ruler, pencil, craft knife, cutting mat, double-sided tape, scissors, tape, all-purpose glue, tracing paper

Piece of stiff cardboard 14 by 14 inches (35 by 35cm), for the box

Piece of stiff cardboard 12¾ by 12¾ inches (32 by 32cm), for the lid

Piece of craft paper 16 by 16 inches (40 by 40cm), to cover the box

Piece of coordinated craft paper 14¾ by 14¾ inches (37 by 37cm), to cover the lid

2 yards (2m) gossamer ribbon, 2 inches (5cm) wide

Tissue paper

RECIPE: Thanksgiving pumpkin pie

Preheat the oven to 400°F (200°C). Grease a 9-inch (23-cm) pie pan.

1 To make the pie crust, sift the **flour, sugar,** and **salt** into a bowl and stir in the **orange rind.** Using your fingertips, rub in the **butter** until the mixture resembles fine crumbs. Beat the **egg yolk** and **cream** together in a small bowl, then stir into the dry ingredients.

2 Shape the mixture into a ball of dough, then turn the dough onto a lightly floured countertop and knead it until it is smooth. Wrap the dough in plastic food wrap and chill it in the refrigerator for at least 30 minutes.

3 To make the filling, steam the **pumpkin** cubes over a saucepan of simmering water for about 5 minutes, or until tender. Set aside to cool.

4 In a mixing bowl, mash the pumpkin with a potato masher or fork, then stir in the beaten **eggs, brown sugar, spices, salt,** and **molasses.** Beat in the **cream** and **orange juice.** ▶

5 Roll out the dough to line the pie pan, trim the edge, and prick the bottom with a fork. Cover the dough with waxed paper and bake blind in the preheated oven for 15 minutes. Reroll the trimmings and cut them into stars.

6 Pour the filling into the pie shell and arrange the **pecans** on top. Brush the pastry edge with **milk** and arrange the stars around it. Bake in the preheated oven for 45 to 50 minutes, until a skewer inserted in the middle comes out clean. Cool on a wire rack before removing from the pan. ▪▪

GIFTWRAP: Spice-box special

Cinnamon-colored ribbon wrapped around the lid and tied into a filmy bow decorates a box covered in two-tone textured papers.

1 Using the instructions for a square box on pages 6–7, make the box.

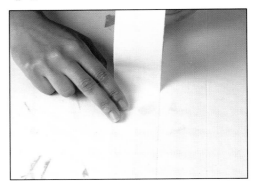

2 Cut strips of double-sided tape and stick them on to the back of both of the craft papers.

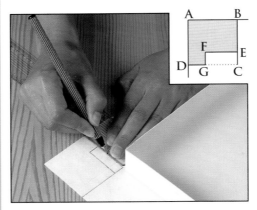

3 Place the lid in the center of the wrong side of the paper. Using the template inset, from one corner, A, measure and mark a square up to the edge of the box, with points B, C, and D. Measure point G the width of the lid sides in from C on the line D-C, then draw in line F-E parallel to G-C and ¾ inch (2cm) from it.

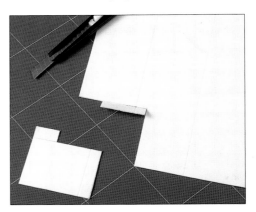

4 Cut out along the line B-E-F-G-D using a craft knife on a cutting mat, and remove that section. Cut along the line E-C and fold the line G-C. Repeat this cutout-and-fold section at the other three corners.

—114—

5 Try folding the paper before removing the tape backing. Place the lid in the center of the paper. At each corner, fold up the side with the flap and bend the flap at right angles. Fold up the other side to cover the flap, and fold in the overlap on both sides to the inside of the box.

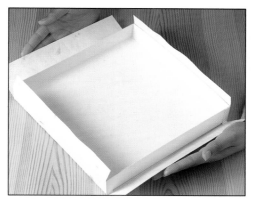

6 To cover the lid with the craft paper, peel off the backing strip, place the lid in the center of the paper and press down on the base to make sure the paper is securely stuck. Then make the folds.

7 Cover the box with coordinated paper in a similar way, placing the box in the center of the paper, marking and cutting away the corner sections to make neat folds. Check that distance G-C is the width of the side of the box.

8 Cut the ribbon in half and cut a 15-inch (38-cm) length from one piece. Wrap that around the lid about 2 inches (5cm) from one side, fold the two ends under, and anchor them to the inside of the lid with tape.

9 Place the shorter length of the remaining ribbon on top of the longer one, with the centers together. Tie the two thicknesses together into a bow (it may help to have something to tie around, such as a pencil). Trim the ends and glue the bow to the ribbon band on the lid.

10 Cut a piece of tracing paper to line the box. Dust the edge of the pie with confectioners sugar, then put it in the box. Place crumpled tissue paper in each corner. ✽

LIGHT-AS-AIR CAKE

CUTTING INTO THIS DELICIOUS CAKE reveals its inner strawberries-and-cream coloring, perfect for a birthday party or afternoon tea. The pansy-covered box adds a summery note.

RECIPE: Light-as-air cake

Preheat the oven to 325°F (170°C). You will need a 7-inch (18-cm) tube pan.

RECIPE INGREDIENTS

6 large egg whites

½ teaspoon cream of tartar

¼ teaspoon salt

1 teaspoon (5ml) vanilla extract

¾ cup plus 2 tablespoons (175g) superfine sugar

1 cup (125g) unsifted self-rising flour

Few drops of pink food coloring

7-inch (18-cm) tube pan

Makes one 7-inch (18-cm) cake

PACKAGING NEEDS

Ruler, string, pencil, scissors, all-purpose glue, tracing paper, craft knife

Round box with lid; the one used here is 9 inches (23cm) in diameter and 4 inches (10cm) deep

2 sheets wrapping paper with floral pattern

Double-sided tape, 2 inches (5cm) wide

At least 24 inches (60cm) thick cord with 2 tasseled ends

Tissue paper, to line box

Small piece of corrugated cardboard, for gift tag

12 inches (30cm) ribbon, ⅛ inch (3mm) wide

1 In a large mixing bowl, using an electric mixer or a hand-held beater, beat the **egg whites** until they are light and foamy. Add the **salt** and **cream of tartar** and continue beating until soft peaks form.

2 Add the **vanilla**, then gradually add the **sugar**, beating between each addition. Continue beating until the mixture becomes stiff.

3 Sift in the **flour** and, using a large metal spoon, fold it into the mixture. Transfer half the batter to another bowl.

4 Add the **food coloring** to the batter in one of the bowls and fold it in with the metal spoon. Stop folding as soon as the color is evenly distributed so you do not break down the air bubbles. ▶

5 Drop spoonfuls of the plain and
pink batters alternately into a
7-inch (18-cm) ungreased tube pan
and smooth the top with the back
of a spoon. (The pan must not be
greased because the cake will fall as
the butter melts.)

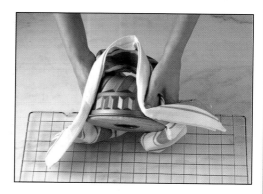

6 Bake the cake in the preheated
oven for 40 to 45 minutes, until a
fine skewer inserted in the center comes
out clean. Invert the pan on a wire rack
and leave to cool before turning out the
cake. Allow the cake to cool completely,
then store it in an airtight container, no
more than 3 days, until you
are ready to wrap it. ▪▪

GIFTWRAP: Heavenly delight

*A deep cardboard box covered with pansy-motif wrapping paper and given
chunky cord handles will endure long after the cake has been enjoyed.*

1 Measure the side of the box to
see how much wrapping paper
you need to cover it. The paper strip
needs to be as long as the circumference
(measure this using string) and as wide
as the depth of the box plus ½ inch
(1.5cm) on each side for overlap.

2 Measure the lid in the same way.
Using scissors, cut strips of
wrapping paper to cover the side of
the box and lid.

3 To cover the top of the lid and
base of the box, draw around
them on the back of the wrapping
paper. Cut out the circles using scissors.

4 Cover the back of the strips and
circles of decorative paper with
double-sided tape. Allow the tape to
overlap the edges where necessary, then
trim to an exact fit with scissors,
taking particular care around
the curves of the circles.

5 Peel the backing off the tape on the larger strip of wrapping paper. Position the box on its side in the center of the paper and smooth the paper around the box.

6 Snip into the overlapping edges with scissors to make them easier to stick down. Fold over the edges, first onto the base of the box and then inside the rim.

7 Cover the base of the box with the decorative paper circle after removing the backing from the tape. Cover the side and top of the lid in the same way.

8 To make handles, cut the cord 12 inches (30cm) from each tassel and knot the free end around the top of the tassel. Glue one handle to each side of the lid, dabbing a little glue on the free end to prevent it from fraying.

9 Cut a strip of tracing paper to line the inside of the box and a circle to cover the base. Line the box with crumpled tissue paper and put the cake on top. Pull up the tissue paper through the center of the cake.

10 Cut out some pansies from the giftwrap and glue them on the lid of the box. (If fresh pansies are in season, you could make a posy instead.) Make a gift tag out of the corrugated cardboard (see page 65, step 6) and glue a cutout pansy to it. Then tie the tag to one of the handles with the ribbon. 🎁

RICH CHRISTMAS FRUITCAKE

BAKED IN A SPHERICAL METAL MOLD, this cake has the appearance of a Victorian-style Christmas plum pudding. A spray of holly or other foliage and berries adds a seasonal note.

RECIPE INGREDIENTS

1¼ cups (150g) unsifted all-purpose flour

½ teaspoon salt

1 teaspoon ground cinnamon

¼ teaspoon grated nutmeg

½ teaspoon ground ginger

½ cup (125g) unsalted butter, at
room temperature

¾ cup plus 2 tablespoons (125g) soft light
brown sugar

2 large eggs

1 cup (150g) golden raisins

1 cup (150g) seedless raisins

½ cup (60g) dried currants

⅓ cup (50g) chopped blanched almonds

Grated rind of 1 orange

About 4 tablespoons (60ml) orange juice

1 spherical mold, 5 inches (12.5cm)
in diameter

Makes one 1¾-pound (875-g) cake

PACKAGING NEEDS

Waxed paper, tape, pencil, scissors,
rubber band

Piece of cotton lining material
20 by 20 inches (50 by 50cm)

Pinking shears (optional)

About 2 yards (2m) wire-edged
ribbon, 1½ inches (4cm) wide

Thin silver-colored wire

RECIPE: Rich Christmas fruitcake

*Preheat the oven to 300°F (150°C). Lightly brush the base and top of a
5-inch (12.5-cm) spherical mold with vegetable oil, then dust them with flour.*

1 Sift the **flour, salt,** and **spices** into a mixing bowl. In another bowl, beat the **butter** and **sugar** with a wooden spoon until the mixture is pale and creamy.

2 Beat the **eggs** one at a time into the creamed butter and sugar, adding about 1 tablespoon of the flour mixture and beating well to prevent the mixture from curdling.

3 Using a large metal spoon, gradually fold in the remaining spiced flour mixture until it is thoroughly incorporated.

4 Stir in the **dried fruits,** chopped **nuts,** and **orange rind.** Add just enough of the **orange juice** to give a thick dropping consistency. ▶

5 Spoon the mixture into the base of the prepared mold. Close the mold and bake it in the preheated oven for 2¼ hours, or until a fine skewer inserted through the hole in the top of the mold comes out clean.

6 Leave the cake to cool in the mold, then unclip it and turn out the cake onto a wire rack. When the cake is completely cool, wrap it in foil and store it in an airtight container until you are ready to giftwrap it. ▪▪

GIFTWRAP: Crisp cotton

Wrap the Christmas cake in plain cream cotton and make a statement with the bow. A collection of cakes, all with different ribbons, looks fabulous under the tree.

1 Remove the foil wrapping from the cake. Rewrap the cake in waxed paper, keeping the shape as round as possible.

3 Place the wrapped cake in the center of the trimmed cloth and draw the sides of the cloth over the top of the cake.

2 Draw and cut sweeping curves from the corners of the cotton. If you wish, cut all around the edges with pinking shears, to prevent fraying and to give a decorative finish.

4 Ease the excess material into even folds and hold the cloth tightly in place with the rubber band. Cut a 10-inch (25-cm) length of ribbon and tie it around the band to hide it.

5 To make a bow to decorate the package, start by forming a 5-inch (12.5-cm) loop about halfway along the remaining ribbon.

6 Holding the loop between the thumb and index finger of one hand, cross one end of the ribbon over to form an X-shape at the center, making a second loop.

7 Continue crossing the ribbon over at the center in this way, using first one end of the ribbon and then the other, until you have made three loops on each side.

8 Bind the center of the bow with the thin wire to secure it, then bind it onto the ribbon around the top of the cake.

9 Adjust the bow to distribute the loops evenly and to conceal the wire. Trim the ribbon ends neatly with scissors. ✤

Note

Instead of using the circular mold, which can also be used to make an ice cream bombe, the mixture can be baked in an earthenware flowerpot. Scrub the flowerpot well and leave it to dry. Then line it with waxed paper lightly brushed with oil and dusted with flour.

TEMPLATES

If you are short of time, or want a more visual aid, here are templates for making some of the more unusual boxes in the book. Each template is shown at exactly half the size of the package; the measurements represent the actual size. Once you have made a box or two, you will be able to adapt the template measurements to suit anything you'd like to package. (To make square or round boxes, see the instructions on pages 6–7 and 8–9, respectively.) ❧

SCOTTISH SHORTBREAD

(pages 12–15) *You will need a piece of medium-weight cardboard 10 by 17 inches (25.5 by 43.5cm). Draw the template onto the cardboard, following the given measurements. For a reusable template, transfer the outline onto graph or tracing paper, then draw around it on the cardboard. Alternatively, photocopy the template at 200% to give the exact size (you may need to tape two or more sheets of paper together).*

To make up the box, score all the fold lines, then follow steps 5 and 6 on page 15.

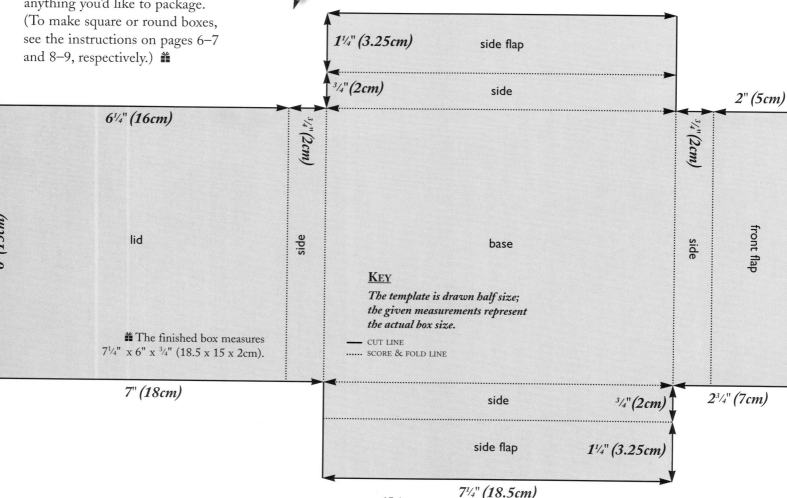

1¼" (3.25cm) side flap

¾" (2cm) side

2" (5cm)

6¼" (16cm)

¾" (2cm)

¾" (2cm)

6" (15cm)

lid

side

base

side

front flap

KEY

The template is drawn half size; the given measurements represent the actual box size.

—— CUT LINE
····· SCORE & FOLD LINE

❧ The finished box measures 7¼" x 6" x ¾" (18.5 x 15 x 2cm).

7" (18cm)

side ¾" (2cm)

2¾" (7cm)

side flap 1¼" (3.25cm)

7¼" (18.5cm)

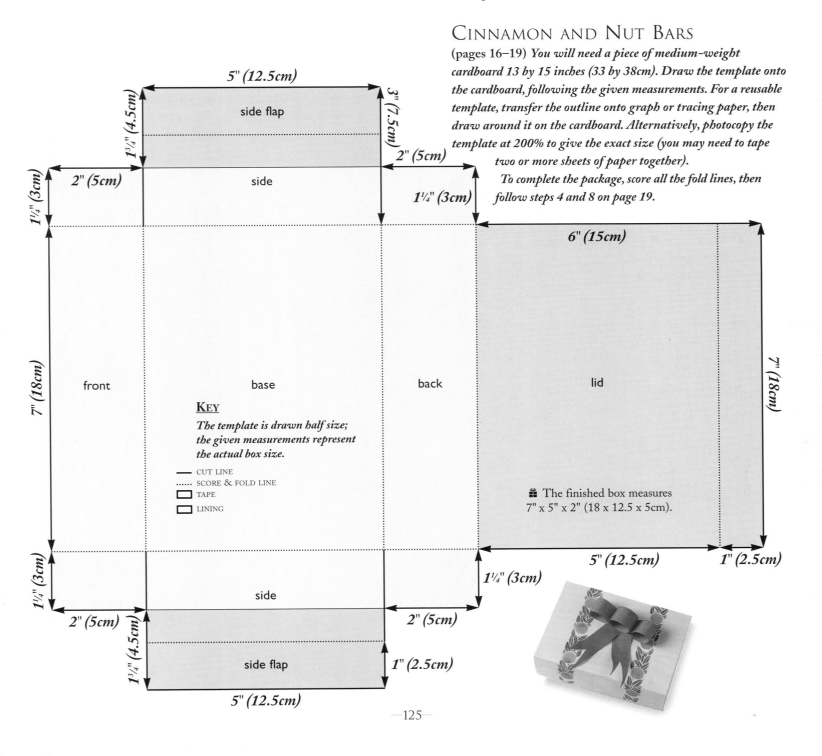

CINNAMON AND NUT BARS

(pages 16–19) *You will need a piece of medium-weight cardboard 13 by 15 inches (33 by 38cm). Draw the template onto the cardboard, following the given measurements. For a reusable template, transfer the outline onto graph or tracing paper, then draw around it on the cardboard. Alternatively, photocopy the template at 200% to give the exact size (you may need to tape two or more sheets of paper together).*

To complete the package, score all the fold lines, then follow steps 4 and 8 on page 19.

5" (12.5cm)

3" (7.5cm)

side flap

1¾" (4.5cm)

2" (5cm)

2" (5cm)

side

1¼" (3cm)

1¼" (3cm)

6" (15cm)

7" (18cm)

7" (18cm)

front

base

back

lid

KEY

The template is drawn half size; the given measurements represent the actual box size.

—— CUT LINE

····· SCORE & FOLD LINE

☐ TAPE

☐ LINING

✤ The finished box measures 7" x 5" x 2" (18 x 12.5 x 5cm).

5" (12.5cm)

1" (2.5cm)

1¼" (3cm)

1¼" (3cm)

side

2" (5cm)

2" (5cm)

1¾" (4.5cm)

side flap

1" (2.5cm)

5" (12.5cm)

Sugar-Frosted Fruits *(pages 82–85)* *You will need a piece of medium-weight cardboard 6¾ by 11⅝ inches (17.3 by 29.8cm) for the box and a piece of thinner cardboard 7⅞ by 12¼ inches (20 by 31cm) for the sleeve. Draw the template onto the cardboard, following the given measurements. For a reusable template, transfer the outline onto graph or tracing paper, then draw around it on the cardboard. Alternatively, photocopy the template at 200% to give the exact size (you may need to tape two or more sheets of paper together).*

To make up the box, score along the fold lines, then follow steps 2–4 and 7 on pages 84–85.

BOX TEMPLATE

¾" *(2cm)*

1⅛" *(2.9cm)*

7⅞" *(20cm)*

10⅛" *(25.8cm)*

side

base

side

KEY

The template is drawn half size; the given measurements represent the actual box size.

—— CUT LINE
····· SCORE & FOLD LINE
☐ TAPE

1⅛" *(2.9cm)*

side

1⅛" *(2.9cm)*   ¾" *(2cm)*   1⅛" *(2.9cm)*

4½" *(11.5cm)*

SLEEVE TEMPLATE

top

4⅝" *(11.75cm)*

side

1¼" *(3cm)*

12¼" *(29.5cm)*

base

4⅝" *(11.75cm)*

❀ The finished box measures
7⅞" x 4⅝" x 1¼" (20 x 11.6 x 3cm).

side

1¼" *(3cm)*

½" *(1.5cm)*

7⅞" *(20cm)*

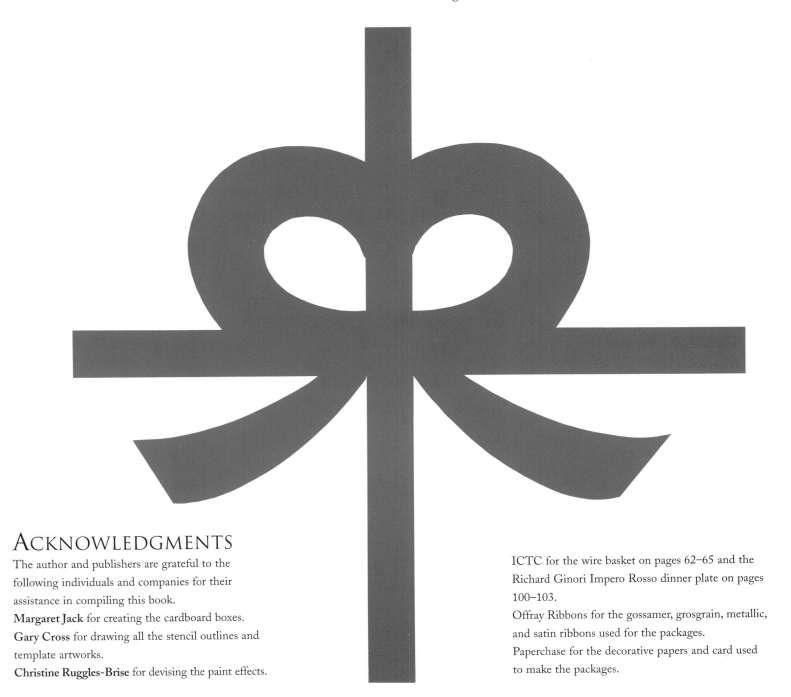

ACKNOWLEDGMENTS

The author and publishers are grateful to the following individuals and companies for their assistance in compiling this book.

Margaret Jack for creating the cardboard boxes.

Gary Cross for drawing all the stencil outlines and template artworks.

Christine Ruggles-Brise for devising the paint effects.

ICTC for the wire basket on pages 62–65 and the Richard Ginori Impero Rosso dinner plate on pages 100–103.

Offray Ribbons for the gossamer, grosgrain, metallic, and satin ribbons used for the packages.

Paperchase for the decorative papers and card used to make the packages.

INDEX

A
almond-paste fruits 58–60

B
bags
  gingham 39
  marbled paper 34–35
baskets
  wooden 26–27
  woven 27, 106–7
bows, making 19, 47, 123
boxes
  see folded box
  "matchbox," giant
  ready-made boxes
  recessed box
  round boxes
  square boxes
buns, lemon sugar-crystal 24–26

C
cakes
  chocolate-pecan gateau 92–94
  Christmas fruitcake 120–22

four-layer spice 108–10
gingerbread 96–98
Italian chocolate fruitcake 104–6
light-as-air 116–18
putting into box 95
rose-petal 88–90
candy, chocolate coconut 54–56
cheesecake, butterscotch-topped 100–3
cheese shells 28–30
chocolate
  -coated nuts 93–94
  coconut candy 54–56
  Italian fruitcake 104–6
  -pecan gateau 92–94
  rum truffles 62–64
Christmas
  fruitcake 120–22
  tree ornaments 39
cinnamon
  and nut bars 16–18
  and sugar bow 110
coconut
  and chocolate candy 54–56
  wreath cookies 36–38
cones, making paper 72–73
containers
  food canister 56–57
  mason jar 76–77, 81
  wire-frame 22–23, 52–53, 64–65

cookies
  coconut wreath 36–39
  ginger and honey 20–22
  vanilla and peppermint 44–46
  Viennese alphabet 32–34
crackle varnish 90–91
cranberry fudge 50–53

D, E
dried lemon slices 26
embossing 76–77

F
fabric
  packages 39, 52–53, 81, 122–23
  paints 52–53
flowerpots 80–81, 123
foil
  embossed 76–77
  wrappers 64–65, 98–99
folded box 18–19
  template 125
fruitcake 120–22
  Italian chocolate 104–6
frosted
  fruits 82–84
  roses and petals 90–91
fruits
  marzipan 58–60
  sugar-frosted 82–84
fudge, cranberrry 50–52

G
gift tags 53, 65, 76–77, 107, 119
ginger and honey fairings 20–22
gingerbread 96–98
  people 40–42
gold leaf, edible 22, 98
gold powder 35, 57

H
honey and ginger fairings 20–22

K, L
kumquat wire ring 102–3
leaves
  pressed 94–95
  stencils 18–19, 77, 80
  sugar-paste 78–80
lemon
  slices, drying 26
  sugar-crystal buns 24–26

M
marzipan fruits 58–60
mason jar 76–77, 81
"matchbox," giant 84–85
  template 126

N
nougat, pistachio 70–72
nuts
  almond-paste fruits 58–60
  and cinnamon bars 16–18
  pecans
    and chocolate gateau 92–94
    in pumpkin pie 112–14
    sugar 'n' spice 74–76
  pistachio
    nougat 70–72
    in Turkish delight 67–68

O
orange and rose-petal Turkish delight 66–68

P
painted packages
  baskets 26–27, 106–7
  boxes 30–31, 38–39, 42–43, 60–61, 90–91, 94–95
  fabric 52–53
  see also stenciled packages

panforte 104–6
paper cones, making 72–73
pecans
  and chocolate gateau 92–94
  in pumpkin pie 112–14
  sugar 'n' spice 74–76
peppermint and vanilla cookies 44–46
personalized gifts 32–35, 74–77
pie, pumpkin 112–14
pistachio
  nougat 70–72
  in Turkish delight 67–68
plate, presentation 102–3
pumpkin pie 112–14

R
ready-made boxes
  round 30–31, 42–43, 90–91, 94–95, 118–19
  square/rectangular 38–39, 60–61, 68–69
  recessed box 14–15
    template 124
ribbon-weave panel 46–47
rose-petal
  cake 88–90
  frosted 90–91
  and orange Turkish delight 66–68
round boxes
  covering 118–19
  making 8–9, 110–11
  ready-made 30–31, 42–43, 90–91, 94–95, 118–19
rum truffles 62–64

S
savory snacks 28–30
sealing wax 73
shortbread 12–14
soft-ball stage test 75
square/rectangular boxes
  covering 114–15
  making 6–7, 46–47, 114–15
  ready-made 38–39, 60–61, 68–69
stenciled packages 18–19, 30–31, 52–53, 80–81, 110–11
stencils
  heart 52–53
  leaves
    and fruit 19
    and nuts 77
    trailing 80
  ribbon-and-bow 127
  shells 30–31
  tulip 52–53
sugar
  -crystal buns 24–26
  -frosted fruits 82–84
  'n' spice pecans 74–76
  -paste leaves 78–80

T
templates for boxes 14–15, 18–19, 84–85, 124–26
truffles, chocolate rum 62–64
Turkish delight 66–68

W
wooden containers
  basket 26–27
  box 30–31, 38–39, 42–43, 60–61